THRIVING
Not Just Surviving

DEPLOYMENT PERSPECTIVES
FOR TODAY'S MILITARY FAMILIES

Editor: Barbara Beye

Designer: Kate Hoyman, Design9Studios

Officers' Christian Fellowship
3784 S. Inca
Englewood CO 80110
www.ocfusa.org

THRIVING
Not Just Surviving

DEPLOYMENT PERSPECTIVES
FOR TODAY'S MILITARY FAMILIES

CONTENTS

DEDICATION

This book is gratefully and lovingly dedicated to our service men and women, and to every military spouse and family member who has ever watched their loved one deploy. In the midst of today's multiple deployments may you thrive and not just survive!

Special thanks to:

Our authors who generously donated their time and creativity to make this book a reality; I pray that your writing has been as inspirational to you as reading your work has been for me.

Cindy Brown and Cindy Wesley—dedicated military wives who brought the ideas and writers together to make this book happen.

Joanna and Dan, Meredith and Matt, and Kim and Tim who shared their deployment perspectives with us throughout this book, with the help of Sarah Hemingway. She graciously interviewed them, then wrote their perspectives for the beginning of each chapter.

Kate Hoyman who prayerfully designed this book after reading every word.

Mike Edwards, Karen Fliedner, and Karen Martin—the OCF publications team.

Officers' Christian Fellowship for giving me time, freedom, and prayer support to work on this book. It has been an honor and a privilege.

—Barbara Beyer, editor

GETTING READY

EDITOR'S NOTE: *We will begin each chapter of this book with a brief interview of Joanna, Meredith, and Kim. Their backgrounds are varied—and so are their views. Enjoy getting to know them and learning from their experiences.*

Preparing for Deployment

What tips can you give on preparing for deployment as a couple?

Joanna: Dan and I went away on a weekend, without the kids, and talked about what our goals were (his for me, ours for the kids, etc.). We chose a theme verse, prayed, talked about expectations and needs. We also talked and prayed about practical things like trips I would take with the kids, basic calendar for the year, and time spent with parents and in-laws. We really wanted it to be a year of "thriving, not just surviving."

Our attitude, and what both of us tried to focus on throughout the deployment, was how we could reach out to others. It's so easy to get caught up in how difficult things are for yourself and get a "woe is me" attitude, but if you focus on how you can help someone else out, and what you can do to serve those around you, it takes the focus off of yourself and makes it easier.

Meredith: Matt and I both felt very strongly that this deployment was the challenge to which God had called our ▶▶▶

Before Matt left we took time together to really talk about expectations.

family. Matt wanted to lead his men with wisdom, courage, and integrity. I wanted to walk through the challenge of caring for our family and the families of our soldiers in such a way as to "give an answer for the hope that I have" in Jesus. We felt very thankful to have this opportunity.

Before Matt left we took time together to really talk about expectations. I also tried to figure out what kind of support I would need. Even though there are lots of good programs in place for free childcare from the Army, the ages of our kids made it exhausting for me to get everyone ready to go, in the car, and in-and-out of the facility. It just wasn't worth it at this stage of life! I knew I needed someone to come into our home for a few hours each week. Matt took that need to our pastor. We were so blessed by the outcome. The pastor's 25-year-old daughter, herself the oldest of five children and the wife of a deployed soldier, volunteered. It was such an encouragement to me, and it filled up her days as well. Every woman doesn't have the same need, but whatever it is (a weekly housecleaner, etc.) it's very helpful if the husband can set that up before he goes. It makes the wife feel really cared for and it's one less thing for her to take care of.

Kim : We look at deployment as a mission field. On his side, he is with a lot of lost and hurting people. It's a time for ministry. I encourage him to look for opportunities to share Christ. I look for opportunities to share with and love the women back here. There are a lot of young wives and mothers experiencing their first deployment, and it's important to reach out to them. Although it is hard to see Tim go, I'm excited to see what the Lord has planned for me. He always has ways for me to learn and grow, and He shows me His love in new ways. There are times I find that I lean on Tim instead of the Lord, so although sometimes it is hard, the Lord brings my focus back to where it needs to be and uses our time apart to remind me to lean on Him. ✪

Preparing the Kids

How do you talk to your children about deployment before it happens?

Kim: I try to keep it upbeat. Kids tend to take on whatever attitude you have. I try to make it an exciting time so my older ones will remember how much fun we had last deployment and look forward to the fun we are going to have this time.

Joanna: Since our kids are young, we tell them that daddy is going to help people in another country. We explained it as if someone were doing something hurtful to someone outside our house and we saw it going on. Would we just sit in our house and pretend nothing was happening, or would we go out there and help the person who needed help? So there are some bad people making things hard for the people over there and daddy is going there to help the good guys. (Not "Daddy's going over there to kill all the bad guys!")

In terms of helping them understand how long he was going to be gone, we used the seasons to explain the time frame. We didn't want to say anything too specific because we had no idea if his deployment would be extended. "It's fall right now and the leaves are changing colors. Soon they're all going to fall off, and it's going to snow and be Christmas, and we'll get to go to grandma and grandpa's house for Christmas and see your cousins! Then it will be spring and the buds will start growing on the trees again. We'll plant flowers and get to play in the rain. In the summer we're going to go to the beach and to White Sulphur Springs, and when the leaves start turning colors again and falling off the trees next time, that's when daddy is supposed to be coming home." ▶▶▶

To our little girls, he gave a special soft doll.

Meredith: Before he left, we would allude to the deployment, but never gave a specific date. For one thing, the exact date changed a lot. But also, because of their ages, they weren't able to understand or cope. It would have just made them sad and anxious. We told them the weekend before he left so they would have some time to process it with him and ask questions but not enough time to dread it. This is also when he gave them special gifts he bought for them before he left. Matt chose these gifts to help them feel like they had a connection to him and to remind them how much he loved them. To our older daughters, he gave a locket with a picture of him with them already in it. To our three-year-old son, he gave a uniform. To our little girls, he gave a special soft doll. These gifts were very meaningful to them throughout the deployment.

What special things did you do as a family before he left?

Joanna: We went camping as a family and spent a week at White Sulphur Springs a month or so before he left. We took lots of family pictures and individual pictures of each kid with dad. I laminated them for each child, and they kept them by their beds.

Kim: We spent as much time as possible together as a family. We enjoyed the time we had before he left and made special memories. We took lots of pictures with daddy so we'd have them to hold onto while was gone. ✪

Saying Goodbye

Joanna: Something to think about is that there will be extended family and friends who want to say good-bye and visit before he leaves. We try to have those visits at least a month out so that our last few weekends are time we get to spend together with just our immediate family.

It's never easy to say goodbye, but there are things we can do to make the transition a little gentler on our youngsters (and us!). I would discourage taking young children to the farewell field when the dads actually leave. There are lots of tears, and kids crying and begging their dads (or moms) not to go. Unless your children are old enough to understand what's going on, it could be a very traumatic experience. Say your goodbyes at home, pray together, then get a babysitter and take him yourself. It gives you those last moments together to hold on to. Allow yourself enough time to go get a cup of coffee or sit in the car and cry for a while before going home to the kids. Give yourself permission to have that time and space and to let the Lord put His arms around you and hold you. ✪

Allow yourself enough time to go get a cup of coffee...

Daddy, I Don't Want You to Go!

by Cindy Wesley, Army wife, Kansas

Tears were streaming down her face. Her daddy said, "What is the matter, honey? Why are you crying?" She said, "Daddy, don't you know?" He said, "No darling, what is it?" She pressed into his big chest and sobbed, "I don't want you to go back!"

Many of us have probably witnessed this with our own children and husbands. I was that little girl many years ago, telling my dad that I didn't want him to go back to Vietnam.

Years later, tears flowed in our house when my husband, Eric, was preparing to deploy to Iraq. The day Eric left will always remain vivid in my mind; as moments ticked away we videotaped Eric with the kids. They clung to him, and we said heart-wrenching things.

War is not fun. Worry, anticipatory grief, and taking care of others all take their toll. Thankfully, Eric returned safely; but he had lost brothers in arms, and some heroic Americans' lives were forever altered due to serious injuries. The human response is to say, "We have served our country and done our duty (the whole family), maybe we need to rethink all of this and consider getting out." Will there be an end to this, or does the Lord want us to continue to do this to our family?

The answer is...*perhaps*. The longer I live, the more I realize that life is not about us, and that most of life is difficult. God will not waste hardship or suffering. First Peter 1:6-7 says, "In this you greatly rejoice, though now for a little while you may have had to suffer grief in all kinds of trials. These have come so that your faith—of greater worth than gold, which perishes even though refined by fire—may be proved genuine and may result in praise, glory and honor when Jesus Christ is revealed."

I want to share a few of the positives that we have experienced as a family when Eric was deployed. I would also like to offer a few words of encouragement.

1. **Our Children Learn that Life is Not About Temporal Satisfaction, and It is Not About Them**

    When we had lost three soldiers in eight days, one of my children complained about something that I couldn't do at the time. I said, "I am sorry; a soldier has just died, and his family is very sad and I need to be with them. You will need to be patient—I can't be with you now." That may sound harsh, but it was the reality of the situation.

Looking back over the last year, I get emotional at what my children have experienced. But I truly believe they were all life lessons that the Lord will use in their lives in a powerful way.

We get into some very good discussions with our oldest children about the geopolitical situation in the world, and what is occurring. They realize that we are in the fight of our lives, much like we were in WWII against the Nazis and fascism, and in the Cold War years against communism. Now it is against Islamic extremism.

2. Going Deeper

I do not wish deployments, danger, or hardship on anyone, but I cherish the sweetness that comes in my relationship with the Lord when Eric is away. We military wives are blessed because we are forced to come to the place that Jesus alone is enough. As I would read Scripture every night, I would pray ▶▶▶

The longer I live, the more I realize that life is not about us, and that most of life is difficult.

the Psalms for Eric and his men. Doing this gave me restful, peaceful sleep, not knowing what the next day might bring. "My presence will go with you, and I will give you rest" (Exodus 33:14).

Listening to praise music and focusing on the Lord in times of difficulty is healing and therapeutic—"Blessed are those who have learned to acclaim you, who walk in the light of your presence, O LORD. They rejoice in your name all day long; they exult in your righteousness" (Psalm 89:15-16).

"Each day has enough trouble of its own," as the Lord said, so I would try to focus on each hour at first, and then each day—one day at a time. If I looked much beyond that I would be overwhelmed with the uncertainty those days could bring. One of my favorite verses that sustained me during Eric's absences, particularly when in combat, is from Lamentations: "Yet this I call to mind, and therefore I have hope: Because of the LORD's great love we are not consumed, for his compassions never fail. They are new every morning; great is your faithfulness" (Lamentations 3:21-23).

3. The Field is Ripe and Souls are Hungry

I wonder what people who don't know Him—and don't have the hope of eternity—do in our circumstances. I am not sure how they survive. But one thing is certain—they are hungry for hope, prayer, words of comfort, and spiritual things.

Use this time to speak into people's lives about the hope you have in Him. Remember there are no atheists in foxholes and none at home either, desperately waiting. We have heard countless stories of men coming to know God and being baptized while in combat. Who is planting seeds with the wives and families back home so that they are receptive to their loved ones' newfound faith? I challenge you to reach out! Help bring a conference to your installation, or offer to start a unit prayer group and open it up to everybody—you may be surprised by who comes. I knew of one young lieutenant's wife in our OCF group at Fort Stewart who invited a different family (the wife and children) from her husband's platoon over every Friday night—no matter who, no matter what rank. That is reaching out, feeding their lives, hearts, and souls—and giving them hope.

Women are hungry to be listened to and drawn out during a combat deployment; they are just as lonely and scared as you are. Let your kids catch your vision of being "Jesus with skin on" to other families.

4. Renew and Revamp

One thing that aided my outlook profoundly was taking time to exercise. Not only did exercise help my physical frame and keep my stress in check mentally, but it also gave me a great time to talk to the Lord and meditate and pray. Many of my friends have used this deployment to go back to college, learned something new, or picked up a new hobby. You will grow and change while your husband is gone—make sure it is for the better. Be intentional about it. Make him proud of how you used the time he was gone.

Final Thoughts

I try to view my husband's being in the military as not just a job but as a calling, and something to which our whole family has been called. This is our portion. And while it might not be the "life of my dreams," it is the life God has given us—all of us in the Wesley family. ✪

Let your kids catch your vision of being "Jesus with skin on" to other families.

Begin With the End in Mind

by Bobbie Simpson, Air Force wife, Washington

Thoughts of reintegration for Larry and me always began before he even left. Looking ahead is a powerful motivator—the childlike mindset of counting down to Christmas, the high school student's thought of college, the young woman's dream of marriage, the young father's hope of one day naming his son. Looking ahead motivates us to live, work, and plan while we wait—and it is the key to living in the present with energy and hope.

When Larry and I had our pre-deployment talks, we focused on coming back together. We envisioned long walks, picnic lunches with the children, standing on the beach and holding hands as we marveled at God's handiwork, silently and verbally thanking God for our reunion.

This looking ahead perspective had its practical side, too. As we purposed to begin with the end in mind, we had to decide what that looked like in pre-deployment, mid-deployment, and post-deployment. This minimized the emotion of departure and separation for both of us. It exposed the frightening unknown.

Practically, looking ahead meant several things. First, we would keep life as normal as possible. Attending church, helping the children with homework, making plans for purchases—we refused to put regular things on hold. Next, we forced ourselves to talk openly about concerns, anxieties, missed celebrations, and the "what ifs." This included talking to the children, bringing them in on the vision for what God might want to do for us—and through us—in this separation, and allowing them to voice their fears. Finally, it necessitated careful thinking and planning. I wrote Larry letters to take with him. Larry wrote notes to the children that they would read later. He recorded himself reading several bedtime stories so we could connect with him as we prepared for bed each night. The children did their part by hiding notes in his socks and books. Because we were actively anticipating our separation, we were not being controlled by it but were cultivating closeness—a unity that would nourish us in the months to come.

The first letter I wrote to Larry characterizes our mid-deployment approach to reintegration. "Keep putting the positive spin on everything. Really get involved with the chapel program. Seek to invest yourself into the lives of other men. What an impact you have made in the lives of the men here! Do that at your deployed location. Be consistent in your Bible time; that encourages us greatly and builds you up. Get aggressive with the must do's (whatever they are). Set goals again—short and long-term—so we can be ready when God shows us what's next. Memorize Philippians 4:8 on the plane." The words I wrote to Larry were ones I had to put into practice myself, a decision which made our time apart productive, and insured that we would stay in pace with each other. Near the end of that first letter I reminded Larry of what a friend had written in his Bible. "No Reserves! No Retreat! No Regrets!" I continued: "Give yourself fully to the work of God there. Don't turn back when things get hard. Move away from regret and on to victory."

Those are good words for us spouses as we face deployment after deployment. Move away from regret. Look to the future victory when you can tell others how God strengthened you.

A unified, optimistic view toward separation will maximize the reintegration process. Three simple ground rules will help.

First, communicate expectations and feelings before his return and routinely after the return. Listen to each other's heart. Really listen.

Next, the mutual exchange of needs, and expectations must happen—without demands. This exchange can be open and friendly. Remember the way we bartered as children: "You do my dishes, and I'll fold your laundry." ▶▶▶

Give yourself fully to the work of God there. Don't turn back when things get hard. Move away from regret and on to victory.

Finally, be willing to give and take, free of grudging and false assumptions. And don't pull rank! Reintegration is no time to "grasp" or demand your rights. Christ did not grasp onto His equality with God but humbled Himself.

Such positive, healthy reunions *are* possible. They happen most often to couples and families who begin with the end in mind, who determine to thrive—not simply survive—during deployments.

But what if the spouse returns physically or emotionally injured? What if either spouse was unfaithful during the separation? What if the heart of one or the other grew tired and cold from going it alone? What if numerous "life events" occurred, which have created a wall between the two? Unexpected troubles of life happen in all marriages! Reintegration will look remarkably different for those with such challenges, but resources are available, and God is near.

Don't quit when your best intentions and plans don't work out. Don't turn back when life gets hard. "'For I know the plans I have for you,' declares the Lord, 'plans to prosper you and not to harm you, plans to give you hope and a future.'" (Jeremiah 29:11) If you say, "Lord, this is not what I expected," His response will be, "This is not the end." ✪

Such positive, healthy reunions are possible.

U.S. Army photo // Matt Button, The Aegis

Keep It All in Perspective

by Dawn Weik Grossman, Air Force wife, overseas

I have the pleasure of working with military children of all ages from Air Force, Army, Marine, Navy, and Coast Guard families. Currently, I am in the classroom molding the minds of kindergarteners. In return, I leave school smelling like tempo paint and bearing gifts such as acorns, feathers, and various forms of artwork.

Children are often solid sounding boards. In their innocence they provide a lot of wisdom, laughter, and perspective. Knowing this, I took the opportunity to ask my students their thoughts about deployment. At five and six years of age, some of these children are in the midst of a parent being deployed for a year or more. Others are "veterans" and have experienced separation in the past. The results were as expected—varied and insightful.

First, I decided to interview "Captain Courageous." Early in the school year he pulled me aside on the playground to tell me his secret; *he is really a super hero.* He flies, conquers just about anything, and is sometimes invisible. I've used this information in the classroom to remind him that super heroes need to know how to read and write. Anyway, this little guy who truly believes he is invincible said, "Deployment is when my Dad goes to a bad place where he might get hurt."

Another child said "I miss my Mom and pray to God she will come home. She's not in a safe place, but I know she will be okay." Then, she launched

> ...he pulled me aside on the playground to tell me his secret; he is really a super hero.

into a Sunday School song with a theme about her faith—a little off key, but showing her grasp of Providence in all situations. ▶▶▶

Others identified deployment as "where my dad works; a place to fight someone; a very long TDY/TAD; when my mom can't come to my birthday party; and somewhere there is shooting." Many simply accept and acknowledge that deployment is a way of life—part of their military life. It touched me deeply to discover that some children also understand that not all real-life situations will end positively. Friends have moved because a military parent was wounded or killed.

Hearing their thoughts caused me to reflect on my own. My family has experienced deployments, an eighteen-month remote tour with an ocean between us, and a slew of TDYs. Always, the two biggest concerns have been separation and safety. That is still the case and applies not only to my family but the extended military family. Regardless of rank, branch of service, or country, military families share a strong bond that is not quite understood by others.

When my spouse was a downrange squadron commander, some of his Airmen were in hand-to-hand combat. It was their lives or the bad guys. At the same time, a dear friend's husband was also deployed—different service, different uniform, different downrange location. It didn't matter. When my friend visited new widows or wounded military members in the hospital, we shared the anxiety and pain. We were "battle buddies" and were in contact routinely. I was her sounding board and she was mine. Having each other was a literal God-send and helped each of us through challenging times. Coming from different military services,

Military kids are smart kids who also understand that life must continue.

we provided one another with a different view. Additionally, I have been influenced by a significant amount of interaction with military members from other countries. My personal motto about deployments is "keep it all in perspective."

Keep it all in perspective—multiple deployments. Some will always have it better than we do and many will have things worse. Downrange some have private sleeping quarters. Some have bunks in cubicles. Some are sleeping on mountain sides. Some active duty members have somehow been through an entire career with one deployment. Others have completed five one-year-or-more stints. Some are on their ninth six-month tour.

Keep it all in perspective—communication. We are not the first, nor the last, to go down this path. During World War II military couples had no email, and few letters or phone calls. For months, wives would not know the well being of their uniformed husbands. They had to rely on limited information via newspaper. Obviously, the ability to communicate has changed dramatically—for the best.

Keep it all in perspective—safety. Our spouse's safety is a daily matter, regardless of being deployed. Whether flying a fighter aircraft, riding his bike through town, driving on a German autobahn, or riding the metro, he could be called home by God at any moment. God is in control. We must trust Him for our loved one's well-being.

Keep it all in perspective—blessings. There is much to be thankful for. One blessing is our incredibly caring military family. We owe much to Americans from all services, civil servants, and contractors.

Keep it all in perspective—life goes on. Captain Courageous and his kindergarten peers accept dangers, acknowledge that separation is a part of present day life, and understand that Providence exists. Those are all significant matters around which to wrap one's brain—especially if one can't even write the entire alphabet. Military kids are smart kids who also understand that life must continue—learning to read and write by day, and saving cities from monsters by night. ✪

SCRIPTURES

Genesis 31:49
May the Lord keep watch between you and me when we are away from each other.

Joshua 1:9
Have I not commanded you? Be strong and courageous. Do not be terrified; do not be discouraged, for the Lord your God will be with you wherever you go.

Psalm 139:7-10
Where can I go from your Spirit? Where can I flee from your presence? If I go up to the heavens, you are there; if I make my bed in the depths, you are there. If I rise on the wings of the dawn, if I settle on the far side of the sea, even there your hand will guide me, your right hand will hold me fast.

Proverbs 16:3
Commit to the Lord whatever you do, and your plans will succeed.

Proverbs 22:3
A prudent man sees danger and takes refuge, but the simple keep going and suffer for it.

Ecclesiastes 4:12
Though one may be overpowered, two can defend themselves. A cord of three strands is not quickly broken.

Jeremiah 29:11
"For I know the plans I have for you," declares the Lord, "plans to prosper you and not to harm you, plans to give you hope and a future."

Matthew 19:13-14
Then little children were brought to Jesus for him to place his hands on them and pray for them . . . . Jesus said, "Let the little children come to me, and do not hinder them, for the kingdom of heaven belongs to such as these." When he had placed his hands on them, he went on from there.

1 Thessalonians 5:24
The one who calls you is faithful and he will do it.

STAYING CONNECTED

Staying Connected Spiritually

During the deployment how do you stay connected spiritually? How do you take care of yourself spiritually?

Joanna: It is definitely good to share prayer requests with each other. Many couples I know have been able to download sermons from church and talk about them throughout the week. It is good to find something you can both read or work through (a devotional or Bible study) if he has time. Some couples use the same daily devotional books so that they're reading the same Scriptures each day.

Having an OCF small group or Protestant Women of the Chapel (PWOC) Bible study group is vital. God didn't create us to go through challenging times alone—and these groups understand. They are a wonderful encouragement. We all have good days and bad ones, and sharing these times with sisters and brothers in Christ is a huge help. Coming back to God's Word really helps keep us looking to Him.

It's hard not to be "too strong" and independent, to find the balance between "Hoo-ah!" and "Help!"

Kim: We pray for each other a lot. We consistently ask each other about prayer needs. I am always asking for prayer about a particular situation or for one (or more!) of our children. I spend time in the Word and prayer, and we go to church when everyone is healthy. I serve where I can in our fellowship. God fills my cup. Sometimes it gets pretty empty before I realize it, but then I hit my knees and ask Him to fill it again. It's hard not to be "too strong" and independent, to find the balance between "Hoo-ah!" and "Help!" I've finally realized I don't have to do it all on my own. ✪

What I Meant to Say Was . . .

E-mail can be wonderful, but it can also be hurtful if you send it before you think. Phone calls can be great or frustrating. Do you have any communication advice, guidelines, or ground rules you follow as a couple?

Joanna: In e-mailing or chatting, things can easily get misconstrued and feelings hurt. We need to be as straightforward as possible, and try not to beat around the bush or play games. Our guys are tired, and things don't always relay well across the ocean.

In the tough or angry times it's helpful to journal. After you've had some time to process and cool down a little, try to communicate some of that to him in an e-mail. It's also important not to harbor bitterness or let things build up. Keep short accounts and "clear the air" (in love!) whenever necessary to avoid a blowup. Continue to talk about expectations, especially about communication (how often, how long) and other "ground rules" for the deployment. His situation may be in constant flux so it's helpful to know what he can or can't do.

Kim: Sometimes it's frustrating because you can't always tell what the other's intentions were for writing things. When you're talking with someone, you can hear his or her tone of voice, but not so much in e-mail. If you need to vent, it's better to hit "delete" than "send." Keep your communications covered in prayer.

Meredith: I used e-mail to share with him as much as I could—what we were doing, funny things the kids said, what God was teaching me, what I was thinking about. I didn't want us to be strangers when he came home. I knew we would both be changing during our year apart, and I wanted us to be a part of each other's lives as much as possible. But I also had grace for him too, knowing that the challenges of deployment were demanding. I tried not to make too many demands on him. But I did savor the notes where he shared what he was thinking and learning.

What wisdom do you have for sharing the "down times" with your husband while you're apart? Any tips for discerning how much to share when you're down and what/when not to share?

Kim: I really value his wisdom and insights, and I treasure his counsel and advice. I do share some of my down times with him, and then he knows where I am and how to pray for me. I also know that he has a lot on his mind and needs to keep his head in his work, so I try not to worry him with the things that are trivial and will work themselves out.

Joanna: It's definitely a hard balance. He wants to hear about what's going on (especially with the kids) but not about all the problems he can't fix. It's hard for him to feel like you're having a really difficult time when there's nothing he can do about it. On the other hand you don't want to pretend it's a breeze and everything is perfect. Be real, but be careful not to overwhelm him with problems. When he has done or said something that was helpful to you, he needs to hear about those things. It will make him realize he's encouraging you, even though he's far away. ✪

In e-mailing or chatting, things can easily get misconstrued and feelings hurt.

You Have to Laugh

What are some ways you've shared humor during deployments?
Funny things you've done to make your sweetheart laugh?

Kim: When you have seven children, you have to have a really good sense of humor. I love to share stories of the day over e-mail. If something funny or one of those "it-will-be-funny-later" things happens, I often take a picture to send along with the story.

Meredith: We sent a lot of care packages. My husband's love language is gifts, so I decided to send him a package every week. When I was out doing errands, I was thinking of him and what he would like. It kept him on my mind. At the commissary I'd look for fun new food things I could send in the mail. I would shop for him at book sales, thrift stores, and clearance sections. I had a bin where I would keep my treasures. The post office has flat rate boxes that I kept on hand. On Thursday night I would put together a box and include pictures the kids had made or notes for him, photos and videos of them—things to keep us in his thoughts every day. The post office was the first stop I made on my Fridays out. It kept me thinking about him and it reminded him how much we love him.

One time we included "ourselves" in a care package. We used butcher-block paper and made tracings of each one of us, just to remind him of how big each child was getting. When he got them, he hung them on the wall and took pictures of himself with us and sent them to us. He called them "A Day with My Family."

Joanna: For Dan's birthday I organized a "poem scavenger hunt." I sent clues to different people in his company, with funny little birthday presents. As each one gave their gift to him, it led him to the next one. At the end of the hunt he unwrapped a life-sized poster of me dressed in full Army gear, along with the last poem:

"Though the Army won't let me come over there,
Know that I'm with you in thought and in prayer.
And when the enemy presses in hard to attack (that is, Satan),
Just smile and remember, 'My wife's got my back!'"

I wanted him to know that I was supporting him in the best way I could, and that I was fighting for him in prayer. It was a fun birthday for him, and his buddies enjoyed being a part of the plot! ✪

My husband's love language is gifts, so I decided to send him a package every week.

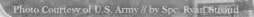

Let's Talk about R & R

Not everyone has a chance for R & R during a deployment, but for those who do, there must be some wisdom learned from your experiences. Did you make a plan? What can you tell us?

Joanna: We decided not to tell the children when Dan was coming home for R & R. They knew that other dads had been coming back for a couple weeks at a time, but I never let on that he was coming. A friend watched the kids when I went to pick him up, and just the two of us stayed away for two nights. (I knew that as soon as the kids saw him, I wouldn't have him to myself the rest of the time!) When we went to pick them up, they were totally surprised. We did plan a vacation to the beach while he was home and made sure the kids knew that daddy just had a vacation for a little while and when we went home he was going to have to go back for a while before he came home for good. It worked out really well because that way, he didn't get back into our routine at home making it harder to have to say goodbye a second time. I was so thankful that a friend suggested that to me.

Meredith: During R & R we found it really helpful to have someone watch the children so that I could pick him up at the airport alone. We had two days together before we came home. It was wonderful! This gave us time to reconnect and talk. And it gave him time to readjust slowly. Then we were both ready to give the kids our undivided attention when he came home to them.

We asked his parents to watch our children while we were away. We thought it would give them a chance to see him too. In retrospect, that was probably not wise. We really wanted our family time, and even though we had invited them, we really wished it had been just our immediate family. When he came home at the end, we invited no family members, and we all were there at the hangar to welcome him home. There's nothing like a reunion! ✪

God's Plans Prevail

by Christy Kaiser, Marine wife, North Carolina

I gave Dan one last kiss goodbye. With a lump in my throat, I thought of all the things he would miss while he was deployed. Most importantly, he'd miss our first child's birth and all the other firsts that come in the beginning of a baby's life. As I waved goodbye, with my eyes swelling with tears and my hands resting on my very pregnant belly, I felt the arms of God wrap around me like never before. Jeremiah 29:11 took on a whole new meaning: "'For I know the plans I have for you,' declares the Lord, 'plans to prosper you and not to harm you, plans to give you hope and a future.'" I climbed into my car alone, shut the door, and buckled my seat belt. I was embarking on an incredible journey.

Three months later, I rushed our four-week-old son, Peter, to the hospital with bleeding colitis. I sat waiting in the emergency room holding onto fear and a screaming baby. What exactly were those plans that God had for us? As I asked the questions, God had answers. A man who looked exactly like my brother-in-law sat down next to me. He, too, had been deployed when his daughter was born. His presence and experience encouraged me. It was a reminder that God had a plan.

With Dan gone during the holiday season, I spent a lot of time with the wives from his squadron. When they would ask, "How are you surviving these months without your husband?" I would say that God was carrying me, and share stories of His faithfulness.

Two days before Dan was to return, Peter was up all night crying with an ear infection. As I paced the hallway trying to comfort him, I felt completely alone. Dan no longer had access to a phone, so as I fell to my knees in prayer at four a.m., I figured he couldn't rescue me with a call. Just as I whispered the words "God help me," the phone rang. It was Dan. He loved me, he didn't want me to worry, and he would be home soon.

God's plans were to show us through the tears and lonely nights what it means when He says that His strength is perfected in our weakness. Just as He promised in Jeremiah, God was there when I needed Him.

I don't know when Dan is leaving again or how long he'll be gone, so I hold on to the lesson I learned from the last deployment: it is God's plan that prevails. He wants to use us, and our life stories, for His glory. ✪

Double Duty for a Solo Spouse

by Marshéle Carter Waddell, Navy wife, Colorado

America is an exhausted, frenzied, sleep-deprived nation on a senseless, ruthless treadmill speeding headlong into tomorrow's to-do list. Our calendars stay so packed with so much activity that we don't even really know how tired we are. We sense that something isn't right, but we haven't had the time or energy to figure it out.

There are many reasons why women in particular are tired to the bone. Many of us are often alone in life's responsibilities and are forced to carry the load solo. Military spouses, like civilian spouses married to businessmen who travel constantly, face weeks, months, and years of keeping the home fires burning by themselves.

There is one guarantee in the life of a military wife: Everything that can possibly go wrong will and usually does within hours or days of the husband's departure. For instance, within the first four days of one of my husband's deployments, the car died in the middle of a lonely, eight-mile stretch of towering green, Hawaiian sugar cane; I discovered a ten-pound rat had taken up residence in my kitchen; the air conditioner unit fell in through my bedroom window in the middle of the night (explain those physics!), and the plumbing system coughed, gagged, then spewed forth a grotesque fountain of sewage from every sink, tub, and shower drain throughout the entire house, while base housing's emergency maintenance hotline stayed busy for over an hour!

I have one question: why does none of this craziness happen when my husband is home? When he is around life seems to stay on the same predictable plateau. The moment he departs, the winds shift and gusty weather moves in.

I mean that quite literally. The only hurricanes that have decided to move inland did so when Mark was twelve time zones away from us. As a result I learned how to board up and duct tape the doors and windows of my house and map out the city's evacuation route.

Parenting has no pause button. The show goes on. I remember photographing my three children's faces up close to send to Mark when they all came down with extreme cases of chicken pox. I wanted him to see a glimpse of the "bonding experience" we had all endured for eight weeks.

I also have had the dubious honor of answering *the* question for all three children over the years—the birds and the bees question. The time for discussing the facts of life arrived on the scene only when Mark wasn't.

Life's everyday demands are enough for a wife who is left behind to man, or should I say woman the oars. Add inclement weather, viral infections, the kids' attempts at mutiny, keeping the house from falling apart, and the bouts of loneliness—and she has all the ingredients for the recipe of resentment.

Along the way, women sometimes lose their soft, feminine side as a result of weathering life's storms alone for too long. They were torn from their moorings of gentle strength and are now sailing at top speed toward becoming old, disheveled, gruff, sarcastic women. I've looked in the mirror and seen that woman looking back at me more than once.

There is only one agent of change that can reverse the negative effect this military lifestyle can have on the beauty and femininity of a woman. *Recognize and rely on Jesus Christ's total sufficiency for every challenge.* He is in control, and allows the faith-building circumstances into my life so I will learn to draw from Him the strength, wisdom, and love I need for every situation. Every trial comes with His guarantee that *He is enough*, that His grace will be there the moment I need it.

God encourages me, "Let us not become weary in doing good, for at the proper time we will reap a harvest if we do not give up" (Galatians 6:9). I find strength and rest in Him alone. Jesus said, "Come to me, all you who are weary and burdened, and I will give you rest" (Matthew 11:28).

I am realizing that I am not left alone to bear the burdens by myself. His name is Immanuel: God is with me. He has offered to carry my yoke in exchange for His, which is "easy and light" (Matthew 28:30). I am convinced He is aware of my needs even in the most trying, seemingly deserted moments. I know from experience that He stands ready and willing to meet those needs. ✪

I discovered a ten-pound rat had taken up residence in my kitchen.

God Is In Control

by Connie Masotti, Army wife, Colorado

My husband's last deployment was to Afghanistan on a Military Transition Team (MiTT). A MiTT assignment is an individual assignment on a team of twelve-to-seventeen service members. They live with the soldiers or policemen they are training during the assignment. My husband and I had both prayed and felt this was the best assignment for him. We had looked at the web site about MiTT teams. We had looked at possible posts where we wanted to PCS because we could have our choice of a follow-on assignment. We had decided that I would move to the follow-on post while he was deployed. I knew there would be only a virtual Forward Readiness Group (FRG). But I had called Fort Carson and knew they had a strong Protestant Women of the Chapel (PWOC) group and that would be my support. I thought I had it all under control—but I would soon learn that only by placing God in that control position, did I stand a chance of making it through this deployment.

With the early move, the three months at Fort Riley, Kansas, for training, then a twelve-month deployment, I only saw my husband for seven weeks out of eighteen months. The virtual FRG that the team leader's wife and I had set up fell apart when my husband's team reached Afghanistan and they were split up. When I contacted the new team leader about starting a virtual FRG he wasn't interested.

I had a chance to meet the soldiers on my husband's team very briefly over the four days that he had at Fort Riley before he deployed. That was great because I am a people person and very visual, so I struggle to pray for people when I can't put a face to the name. The one person I got to know very well was my husband's battle buddy. However, he was killed by a sniper six months into the assignment. I will forever remember that soldier's smiling face waving to me via the Internet.

I struggled mightily with the fact that there was no information coming out about what my husband was doing over there. My husband didn't feel safe discussing anything with me, even once it was on the news. I am the type of person who loves the news, the facts, and being "in the know." So I was making my poor husband miserable trying to understand what was happening in the area he was serving.

And of course, it wasn't until I finally realized how miserably I was failing at trying to control the situation that I turned it all over to God—and it became bearable.

I would get on the Internet and look at news stories about the area where my husband was and think, *Wow, he might have been in on that.* I helped start an e-mail roster of Colorado spouses with service members on a MiTT team or other individual assignments.

And when my husband's battle buddy was killed, and I saw my husband struggling with guilt, God reminded me to pray, pray, and pray again for more than just my husband's safety from bullets and IEDs.

At PWOC, we were doing a wonderful study on the book *For Women Only*. My husband and I studied that book and then *For Men Only*. That gave us things to talk about when he could call or get on the web cam.

And then I asked my pastor about ways the church could reach out to the military. It turned into a Military Ministry Team—of which I am the leader. That was never my intent. I didn't feel that I had the necessary qualifications; however, God has provided.

I wish I could say that I've learned my lesson and will always automatically turn control over to God in every circumstance. In the past my theme song has been, "God's Still Working On Me." I'm asking Him to make my new theme song, "God Is In Control." ✪

God reminded me to pray, pray, and pray again.

A Senior Spouse's Thoughts

by Dawn Phillips, Army wife, Missouri

I dealt with a lot of anger during my husband's first deployment because he wanted to go to war and I felt that he didn't want to hear about my feelings. I also was dealing with some serious health issues and my husband was worried that they would keep him from deploying. During that deployment, I dealt with some tough situations with two girls in college and a son in high school.

Once deployed, I felt like my husband wanted me to "be happy" every time he called. I knew that he had a lot of weight on his shoulders, but I really had no one else I could talk to. He had been my closest friend and support for years. I felt quite alone when he left.

My husband was a brigade commander and I was responsible for looking after all the spouses in the brigade. I knew they were dealing with hard issues as well and I really wanted to be there for them. I tried to be strong and support them, while silently dealing with my own issues. I would leave the ladies little gifts by their door so they would know someone cared about them. But I never felt I was doing enough though, and that was hard on me.

God *was* there for me the whole time and I would run to Him—but I had a lot of anger issues, too. After my husband came home it took us a year to work out my anger issues and it took him two years before he finally felt back to his old self. He felt responsible for the death of all fifteen of the soldiers under his care who had died. He saw many things no one should have to see and survived many attacks meant to take his life.

During that time I tried my best to get back closer to God. I used to be so close to God that I would talk to Him all day long. I cherished my relationship with Him. Now I tried praying more and reading the Bible more, but I felt myself slipping away from God, and I felt hopeless to stop it. I cried out to God to help me—knowing that the helping might be painful. That is how much I missed the closeness I had shared with Him.

For my husband's second deployment, he was hand-selected to be on a special team. Though honored to be chosen, he was very upset about leaving me again. All of our children were gone from home by now, so it would be just me. We were blessed to have one of the big houses on post—joking that the Army gives you these big houses when your kids are all grown and gone.

Day after day I sat in that big house by myself with my two dogs and my cat. I thought people would stop in and check on me, to see how I was doing. But only a few people did at first—and then no one came after the first month. I felt abandoned. My children were worried about me. One day I opened my front door and there stood my daughter! She had flown in to surprise me and stayed with me three days. I will always treasure that.

I asked my husband to share the hard times and scary times with me because while I knew he needed to be strong for his men, he also needed to talk to someone. I felt this was very important so that when he returned home, I would have an understanding of what he had been going through. It was very difficult for me to relax knowing he was over in Iraq working sixteen-hour days. I could hear the raggedness in his voice.

On the second Easter day of my husband's deployment I got a phone call from him. It was the middle of the night for him and he was huddled on the floor of his trailer with all his battle gear on. So many rockets were coming in that he had pulled a mattress over his head and called me. He said they had one-hundred-ninety-four rockets come in at them in a three-day period. There were many nights when he hardly got any sleep. No place was safe. His spirits were at an all-time low. It seemed to me that just about every good Iraqi that he had worked with had been killed. Every time a soldier was wounded my husband would visit him. He flew to every MP memorial service. ▶▶▶

I cried out to God to help me—knowing that the helping might be painful.

One day he called and I could tell he had tears on his face. He said a rocket had exploded in the gym, killing two men he worked closely with and wounding eighteen others. My husband was the one who had to identify their bodies. With tears in his voice he said that his friends were so wounded that he couldn't even make out their faces and he had to identify them by using their dog tags. What does a wife say to that?! I gave him as much comfort as I could and then I ran under God's wings and hid my head and cried. Every Scripture verse that came to my mind was about God protecting His children under His wings. I pictured myself huddled next to God and that got me through those nights.

I want all military spouses to know that even though I am a senior spouse, I face many of the same things they do. I do not consider—or even know—what rank a spouse's husband is. It does not matter at all to me. We are women who love our husbands, and our country. We are sisters because of what we share. Our bond is strong because we experience so much of life and death together. We understand what it is like to be alone. We understand that when we are at our lowest depths and feel like we cannot go one more day God shelters us under His wings and gives us the comfort that only He can give. ✪

Our bond is strong because we experience so much of life and death together.

Share My Calling

by Anne Borcherding, Army wife, Kansas

"This isn't just a job for me. This is my calling, and I need you to share my calling." As he described his commitment to the Army, my husband's voice was filled with emotion. It grabbed my attention. Rob and I were attending an intensive marriage retreat before the first of three deployments. God opened my eyes that day to an essential element of both Rob's service in the military and our marriage.

When Rob shared his vision with me, I would have described myself as supportive of his career. I understood a fair amount about the military, had attended countless functions, and attempted to make the most out of each move. I had also "grown up in Officers' Christian Fellowship" so I believed I viewed the military as a mission field. Wasn't all that enough? What else did he need from me?

A calling is defined as "an objective or task that somebody believes is his or her duty to carry out or to which he or she attaches special importance and devotes special care." Accordingly, a professional calling goes beyond earning a living; it connotes a passion. When we view military service as a joint calling, it alters our view of circumstances and challenges. Sharing a passion gives rise to a vision of something greater. Deployment is no longer something to be endured but a piece of a bigger picture.

I did not immediately embrace the idea of a shared calling. It was a process. Initially I thought, "I love my husband, I am there for him, but the military is *his* calling not mine." However, God began to open my eyes to a different outlook.

- First, He showed me that I had possessed a critical and selfish spirit about the military. I had thought far more about how Rob's career affected me than what it might mean to him. This attitude had wounded his spirit.
- Second, God revealed to me how integral a man's profession is to his identity. When I criticized the military, I was criticizing Rob.
- Third, I was reminded that God had brought Rob and me together (Genesis 2:24). He had a purpose for our union and it wasn't just for our happiness.
- Fourth, His Word instructed me that wives were created to be a man's ▶▶▶

helpmate. In the Hebrew, the word for helper denotes a lifesaving counterpart. God designed wives to be instrumental in helping their husbands carry out their life's mission. I was convicted that sharing Rob's life meant sharing his calling.

Sharing my husband's calling required an attitude adjustment. I had to challenge my thinking regarding some core truths from God's Word. Did I really believe my heavenly Father's promises? I asked myself some tough questions:

- Can I release the plans I have for my life? –Jeremiah 29:11
- Can I truly trust that God is working "all things together for my good?" –Romans 8:28
- Can I give thanks in everything, viewing it as God's will for me? –1 Thessalonians 5:18
- Can I "count it all joy" when I experience trials? –James 1:2
- Can I hold my tongue when I want to be critical of my husband's profession? –James 3:3-9
- Can I be "anxious for nothing" and instead pray with thanksgiving? –Philippians 4:6

Believing God to be true to His Word, I chose to join Rob in his call to military service. Life has not magically become easier. His deployments didn't just fly by, and feelings of frustration haven't disappeared. But, I have a new-found desire to serve, love, and minister to the military community. I am far less irritated by, and more supportive of, the demands his job places on him. My better attitude has also brought a surprise added benefit—an improved relationship with my husband!

I have a new-found desire to serve, love, and minister to the military community.

Days at home without

a spouse can be challenging even when you do share his calling to the military. Following are some ideas to help keep you focused:

1. Have a vision for the deployment. What do you hope to accomplish personally, with your children and in ministry?

2. Look for ways to be involved with the military community. During one of our deployments a friend started a regular prayer night. All family members were invited to join us in praying for our spouses and the war.

3. Pray for ministry opportunities. There are so many needs. Ask God to show you how you can serve others. It always helps to take your eyes off yourself.

4. Stay informed about the location of your husband's deployment. Know what challenges are being faced so you can pray more effectively.

5. Be consistent in seeking God daily.

6. Daily practice gratitude for the ways in which God is blessing you.

7. Be mindful of specific ways to support your spouse. ✪

Rocket Rabe

by Margo Rabe, Army wife, Germany

While stationed in Germany, my chaplain husband was deployed to Afghanistan, and frequently traveled to Forward Operating Bases (FOBs) to visit soldiers. It seemed that everywhere he went, the FOB would receive rocket fire while he was there. He eventually earned the nickname Rocket Rabe.

On one occasion he called me, and we were enjoying a nice chat when I heard a very loud boom through the phone. A bit shocked I asked, "Do you need to go?" After a short pause he said, "Yes, I think I should." I asked him to call me back if he could, and hung up the phone not really feeling fear, but a sense of shock. I bowed my head and prayed for his safety and my comfort. Immediately, I had a sense of calm and peace. I told the children, and we prayed together. I waited for about fifteen minutes and still hadn't heard from him. I had no way of knowing when he would be able to call again. Taking my cell phone, I took the children to the store (which was due to close in half an hour) for some school items they needed the next day. I will admit that at one point the thought went through my head that I could already be a widow and not know it. But even as that thought came, I replaced it with prayer, and the peace was still there. Soon my cell phone rang. I was very glad to hear my husband's voice even when his first words were, "Where are you? I called home and no one answered." I promptly told him where we were and why. He may have thought at first that I didn't care very much about what was happening to him. But I had placed him and his safety in our heavenly Father's hands—and there is no safer place!

I chose to trust my God, and go on with my scheduled plans because:

1. I was trusting God and I had His peace.
2. I had no power to change my husband's situation.
3. I could and did pray.
4. I could complete the task of parenting by providing what my children needed.

Had I stayed at home I wouldn't have met my children's needs. I would have had more time and opportunity to worry. And what message would that have sent to my children about trusting our Savior? To have stayed home and worried would have been to fail my heavenly Father and my children both physically and spiritually. ✪

The Gift of Prayer

by Glenda Clipp, Army wife, Oklahoma

I received a phone call from my mother-in-law late one night during my husband's deployment. There was panic in her voice as she told me she felt like John was in danger and that we needed to have a special prayer for him. She didn't know that I, too, was awake with the same thought. We prayed together on the phone for John's protection. Immediately after I hung up, I called our prayer chain at church, and close family and friends, for an "emergency 911 call to God" on John's behalf.

What we didn't know was, that at the same time we were praying, John was engaged in heavy fire and had gotten pinned down in the streets. A grenade went off under a Humvee parked six feet away from him. I believe with all my heart that our prayers lifted up at that moment kept John from being killed. I learned during his phone call the next morning that the vehicle took most of the blow. He had shrapnel in his thigh and neck, his canteen had shrapnel through it, and his rifle was hit. While he has some extensive hearing loss from this event, I praise God that I still have him.

Throughout deployment, though it was painful not to have my husband home, my prayer life was never stronger. What a blessing! During my husband's deployment, God and I developed an intimate relationship where I relied only on Him to get me through the trying times. When I was lonely, I called on the Lord. When I was hurting, I called on the Lord. When I needed guidance with our two teenagers, I called on the Lord. Don't ever underestimate the power of prayer.

I pray that God will lay it upon our hearts to become prayer warriors. The best gift any military wife could ever give her husband is to pray unceasingly for him. ✪

Safety in War

by Raeann Pajo, Army wife, Virginia

When my husband was slotted to be deployed on a MiTT team, living among the Iraqis, we prayed that the Lord would send him to a safe place. But we quickly learned that nowhere is safe in a war zone. Our safety is in the Lord—no matter where He chooses to place us.

"That day" will always stick out in my mind—never to be forgotten. That was the day I received the phone call every military spouse dreads: my husband had been injured. A notification officer called on Christmas day.

"Mrs. Pajo, your husband was involved in an IED accident and was medevaced to a nearby hospital. He has shrapnel in his left leg, and has been heavily sedated for the pain." He could not tell me if it was just a nick or if Marc would lose his leg—nothing. I asked if he was conscious; he could not verify that. I asked if he would be flown to Germany; again, he could not verify. All he could tell me was that my husband was in a very good hospital.

My heart was in my stomach. "When can I expect to hear from my husband?"

"I don't know. But if he is not in surgery, he will call you soon." Then he told me that another call from him that night would mean my husband's condition had changed for the worse. Although I was shaken, I knew God was with me. All I could think about was *if he dies at least he is a Christian.*

I called my pastor's home and told him about my phone call from the notification officer. He prayed for Marc, and for me to be filled with God's peace. God gave me peace that I cannot explain. He gave me the strength to call my husband's mom.

As the night went on, I prayed. I told God, "I asked You to protect him and You did not!" But I could sense God telling me, "Be still and know that I am God." God was telling me to trust Him—to really trust Him—and not merely to trust that my husband would live and come home to me. God wanted me to trust Him no matter what would happen because He is God Almighty, and He is in control. The night went by without a phone call, so I knew Marc's condition had not worsened.

Finally I received a call that Marc was upgraded from seriously wounded to non-seriously wounded. But there was still no call from Marc. The next morning he called, and began to tell me a little of what happened. Two of his best friends were dead. Hearing my husband's pain broke my heart. It was one of the hardest things I ever had to do. I prayed with him and tried to encourage him to pray so he would not get bitter.

During his recovery in the hospital, the Lord led Marc to the Scripture, "But I tell you who hear me: Love your enemies, do good to those who hate you, bless those who curse you, pray for those who mistreat you" (Luke 6:27-28). Although Marc had read that, it was not what he wanted to hear. It took a while for him to put that into action, but eventually he did.

Going through something like this, you have two choices: to trust God, pray, and grow in Him; or to not trust God, and get angry and bitter. It is easy to go the second route if your prayer life is weak or if you don't have the prayers and encouragement of others. Prayer helped us get through this. We never stopped believing in God because we know He is real and His Word is true, even though we can't understand everything He is doing. I will never understand what my husband has gone through, but I know that God knows. And we need to be sure we are living for Christ, putting Him first.

I have learned that God keeps His promises, and that sometimes God's way of protection is not always what I think it should be. I know that there are no limits when it comes to God's protection. He sees the big picture and makes no mistakes. There is always hope in Christ Jesus. ✪

That was the day I received the phone call every military spouse dreads: my husband had been injured.

Chapter 2

SCRIPTURES

Psalm 141:3
Set a guard over my mouth, O Lord; keep watch over the door of my lips.

Proverbs 12:25
An anxious heart weighs a man down, but a kind word cheers him up.

Proverbs 15:30
A cheerful look brings joy to the heart, and good news gives health to the bones.

Isaiah 52:7
How beautiful on the mountains are the feet of those who bring good news, who proclaim peace, who bring good tidings, who proclaim salvation, who say to Zion, "Your God reigns!"

Ephesians 4:26-27
In your anger do not sin: Do not let the sun go down while you are still angry, and do not give the devil a foothold.

Ephesians 4:31-32
Get rid of all bitterness, rage and anger, brawling and slander, along with every form of malice. Be kind and compassionate to one another, forgiving each other, just as in Christ God forgave you.

Ephesians 5:19-20
Speak to one another with psalms, hymns and spiritual songs. Sing and make music in your heart to the Lord, always giving thanks to God the Father for everything, in the name of our Lord Jesus Christ.

Philippians 1:4-6
In all my prayers for all of you, I always pray with joy because of your partnership in the gospel from the first day until now, being confident of this, that he who began a good work in you will carry it on to completion until the day of Christ Jesus.

Colossians 3:23
Whatever you do, work at it with all your heart, as working for the Lord, not for men.

1 Thessalonians 5:11
Therefore encourage one another and build each other up, just as in fact you are doing.

FROM THE FRONT

The husbands of the three women we've been interviewing speak up to begin this vital chapter.

What advice would you give to couples to help them prepare for deployment in the most positive way?

Tim: I'd say to start preparing for deployment around the six-month mark. It's so important to think ahead, particularly between husband and wife, but also with your children. Generally, your children will like what you like and accept what you accept. If you talk about daddy's upcoming deployment as part of life, I think children become very accepting of it. It doesn't make not having dad around any easier, but before he leaves they'll perceive the transition with the same spirit mom and dad have. Mom can tell them she can handle it and life will continue almost as normal, but if she doesn't believe it with her heart, they will eventually see through the façade. So a key role in helping a husband prepare for deployment is that his wife accepts it as joyfully as possible. That may take some time on your knees asking God to give you that heart because it doesn't come naturally. Having a heart change makes it easier on your children, but it's even more empowering for you, the mother/father/teacher/provider/comforter/leader. The entire family will draw courage and strength from knowing that this time apart is God-ordained.

Matt: I need my wife to help me anticipate/understand the emotional reactions of each family member to the deployment. We found it helpful to think of each person's primary love languages from the book *The Five Love Languages* by Gary Chapman. This understanding helped me to develop a pre-deployment plan to support each family member during my absence. ▶▶▶

I want my wife to be involved with the military pre-deployment stuff. Don't dread the deployment. Don't live with the angst that I'm already gone six months before I leave. Work hard to trust God and your husband that it will be okay. On a practical level, know that I'm going to want/need to buy some stuff before I go—gear for my combat mission or things to help me stay Christ-focused.

Dan: Talk through potential problems: A big help for me was talking about expectations. The guiding principle for resolving conflicts in our family has been to face them as a team. We view conflicts and their sources as something external to our marriage, something we are able to fight against as a team without fighting against each other. This principle is especially true in preparing for deployments. Looking at the problems we felt we might encounter, we tried to talk through as many as possible. In doing so, we covered a lot of challenges that eventually did arise, and we had the benefit of having thought through those things in advance.

Discuss expectations! Distance and lack of communication can really add stress to an already difficult situation. We talked about all kinds of expectations: how often we would talk, what we would talk about, how I could help with kids while half a world away, and how I could stay connected with the kids. We discussed what level of detail I should go into when talking about rough days and what was too much information. Through these conversations and prayer time, we came to an understanding of what we each expected of each other and of our time apart.

Discuss finances! Talk about financial plans ahead of time. Do some research to determine exactly what additional money you'll earn while you're deployed. Once you have done this, make sure you talk with your spouse about how you two wish to use it. Adjust (or create) your budget to ensure that you are doing everything you want to do and you are in agreement about how to use the extra money. Plan some of it for special trips for the family while you're gone, plan some for your personal use while deployed, plan additional savings or whatever else you deem important. Realize also that your financial goals may change after you experience combat and separation from your family for the first time. Discuss with your spouse ahead of time the possibility of re-evaluating finances mid-deployment.

Matt: One thing that really helped our family was to do a detailed planning session before the deployment. One-to-two months prior to leaving would be about right. This was close enough to the deployment to allow fairly good clarity on the details but far enough out so that Meredith knew the plan and could relax and really enjoy the last few months we all had together (see sidebar, next page). Over the remaining weeks the husband can take time to pray and seek out ways to position his family for success during the deployment. Create a signed contract with someone to cut your grass. Coordinate for a monthly or weekly night out for your wife. Buy her a gift certificate for a massage. Talk to your pastor or chaplain about any concerns you have for your family and ask for the congregation's support. Write a letter to your friends and family discussing the upcoming deployment and requesting their prayers during your deployment.

This process was immensely helpful for Meredith and me during our deployment. It communicated my love and concern for our family even before I left. Also, by working through these topics deliberately it allowed all of us to enjoy our last few months together. During the entire deployment the discussions Meredith and I had prior to my deployment helped me continue my role as a husband and father. ▶▶▶

It's so important to think ahead, particularly between husband and wife, but also with your children.

I would recommend that the couple

set aside an evening or even an overnight getaway to work through the following:

1. Start with prayer together and ask for God's wisdom during your time together—much like OCF's *Pray, Discover, and Obey* process.

2. If you have faced deployments in the past, spend some time discussing how things went. Look for the key lessons learned so that you can build on the positives and look for fixes to the negatives. Many of the things that went well on our second deployment were formed in the struggles of our first. As a small example, I learned that a handwritten letter was very meaningful to Meredith.

3. Talk about your concerns for the deployment and ask her about hers. Listen carefully for where she may need help. (Will she need someone to help with lawn mowing or snow removal, help prioritizing the activities she and the children are involved in, help in taking time for herself?) Don't try to "fix" her and her "issues" at this point, just listen carefully.

4. Ask your wife what issues she foresees for each of your children. She will have some deep insights into how they may react to the stresses of the deployment and ideas on how you can help them.

5. Sit down with your calendars and walk through the whole deployment month-by-month. Discuss the major events of the upcoming year. Think through the major holidays. Where will the family spend them and with whom? Talk about any major trips or visits. Who should they visit and who should visit them? (Also talk about who should not visit and/or boundaries). Next, look at an average week and think about if/how it should change while you are gone. To be overcommitted is a huge stress on the family.

6. Finish with prayer.

—Matt ✪

Even though you know God is caring for your family while you're away, what are some things that concern you consistently, things you continue to pray about for your family?

Matt: I prayed consistently that Meredith would be sustained by God's strength as she carried out the roles and responsibilities of both parents. That's a lot of responsibility. And another consistent prayer was that God would meet their needs, both general and specific, through our friends and church.

Tim: Every man stares death in the face, especially a military man going to war. It has to be contemplated and the cost calculated as it relates to "What if I don't come home?"—not necessarily written down—but at least considered.

One of my biggest concerns is for my children, particularly my boys. Boys need a male role model. They need to be tested and approved of, emotionally, spiritually, and physically. These things are important during the middle school years and even more as they come into their teenage years. They want to know that they have what it takes to be a man, and they're looking for an example to follow. Only a man, through God, can validate another man, and I don't want TV or a neighbor to be that man. So I pray often that my absence would not be at a crucial time in their coming of age and that we would be able to pick right back up where we left off. While deployed, I formulate or refine a game plan to be implemented when I return, a plan that leads them onward to Christ and His truths, and away from the lies of this world.

My family's health is also something that consistently weighs heavy on my heart while I am gone. With seven little ones, a common cold can last weeks as it passes around from one to another, and something like the chicken pox could be crippling to a single mom of seven. So I pray for the health of my family and I pray for God to give Kim the stamina to encourage and implement healthy habits.

Dan: When planning for a mission or riding around on a patrol, I might have briefly thought, *I wonder what my family is doing right now?* But in general I would be almost totally focused on the task at hand or those to come in the near future. Thinking in-depth about my wife and kids was ▶▶

more a deliberate action that took place while reading letters, e-mails, or looking at pictures. The things that concerned me most were the times I could tell that my wife was really stressed to her limit with Family Readiness Group responsibilities, extended family pressures, the kids' misbehavior, or my well-being.

Another tough thing was feeling like we were not communicating anything of value on the phone. To deal with this we tried to come up with a method for communicating. We used the acronym K-I-S-S: a Kind word, an Intercessory request, a Spiritual lesson being learned, and a good Story. This helped me prep for phone calls and helped us get more out of our limited time on the phone.

A similar problem was feeling like I was losing touch with my kids. It was very difficult to spend a minute or two trying to just understand what the little ones were even saying or asking "yep" or "nope" questions of the older ones. I recommend talking to your kids about how you want to talk to them on the phone. A few other ideas are to draw pictures that they can color in. Make and send videos to them. Record yourself singing songs and reading books so that you can provide some virtual help with bedtime. ✪

We used the acronym K-I-S-S: a Kind word, an Intercessory request, a Spiritual lesson being learned, and a good Story. This helped me prep for phone calls and helped us get more out of our limited time on the phone.

You've seen some marriages fall apart during deployments and others grow closer. From what you've observed, what are some "do's and don'ts" for couples separated by deployment?

Tim: I think one of the lost arts of communication is that of handwritten letters. It's so hard to sit down and hand-write anything when you can e-mail or use your cell phone to get instant updates from the home front. Letters, particularly love letters, are treasured gifts. Sometimes your emotions and thoughts come through in letters with a clarity that an e-mail rarely conveys. I have saved many letters from my wife, going back and reading them again, hoping to relive the same euphoric feelings they gave me the first time. Sometimes she sprays them so they smell like her. Nothing else makes me yearn for home like that.

One important "don't" would be for the spouse at home not to make any major purchases or life changes (*i.e.* getting a new dog) without talking it over first. Although the deployed spouse is far removed, he still likes to be considered in decisions affecting the whole family. Not consulting the other first could be the catalyst to a rocky road. This is especially unwise just before the return from deployment. At the long-awaited homecoming there shouldn't be anything coming between you when you first embrace—except maybe a little one- or two-year-old. ▶▶▶

Letters, particularly love letters, are treasured gifts.

Dan: Talk about finances ahead of time. Talk about expectations.

Matt: Here are a few "Do's and Don'ts" for keeping your marriage and family strong.

- Do stay connected as much as possible.
- Do send her flowers.
- Do pray for her and the children.
- Do read your Bible and go to chapel whenever possible.
- Do know what's going on in their daily lives (*i.e.* piano recitals, games, doctor appointments) I know you can't "do" anything about it, but you can ask about it and be interested.
- Do send the kids little things that you buy or make.
- Do maintain a pure heart. Find an accountability partner (could be someone stationed with you or at home) to ask you the hard questions.
- Do listen carefully to the details of her life and provide your thoughtful, interested father/husband perspective.

- Don't second-guess her decisions.
- Don't look at pornography.
- Don't get involved in chat/MySpace with any woman except your wife.
- Don't think that she won't find out about something that you do while deployed. "What happens overseas stays overseas" is a myth.
- Don't spend much money. Do you really need it?
- Don't tell her every detail of how you almost got killed. ✪

Do send her flowers.

What is something your wife has done, written, said or sent to you that's really encouraged you?

Dan: Two things come to mind. My wife had a nice birthday surprise for me. My friend in my battalion gave me an envelope that started me off on a scavenger hunt that took me all over our Forward Operating Base. At each stop, I received a poem that was the clue for the next leg of the journey. At the final stop, I was given a huge envelope made of cardboard. The contents? A life-sized poster of my wife wearing full combat gear. I pinned her up on the wall behind my chair in my room and from that day forward, as she had said in her poem, she "always had my back."

The second thing was an alarm clock she sent me that had a recorded message from her in it as the alarm. I opened it, thrilled to hear what it might say. I started the message and then realized that I was in the midst of a bunch of other guys. Thinking the message might be too intimate, I tried to stop it. In the process of fumbling around with the buttons, I ended up deleting the message. I was devastated! I ended up calling her later to see what it had said.

When we had a video chat connection, I played *Simon Says* with the kids because I could see them lined up against the wall opposite the computer. They had a hoot with that, and I got to see the kids have fun, not just talk to them.

Matt: Meredith was great about sending me pictures and videos of her and the kids. I really enjoyed the notes she sent about the funny things the children had said or done. She'd tell me about good times as a family. This didn't make me feel left out; in fact, it boosted my morale and let me know that they were okay.

Another thing she did was to send lots of care packages. Meredith knows my love language is gifts, and she was wonderful about sending packages with small gifts or books, and hand-made pictures/creations from the kids.

Tim: One of the best surprises I found in my bag after deploying was a simple photo album filled with some of my favorite pictures over the years. The album was only half full so that pictures could be added.

Words of encouragement from Kim are always timely and treasured. Her words are caring and relevant, and they get to the heart of the matter. On ▶▶▶

the other hand, my words encourage her when she has had an overly taxing day. I tell her "Be strong and courageous." "Be very strong and courageous."

Kim's saving grace is her sense of humor. Sometimes I get frustrated that she laughs at silly (but very naughty) little children because I think she is encouraging them, but her perspective is one that I—and probably many others—should adopt. She senses when to laugh and when to discipline. Kim's hands are so diligent, regularly demonstrating a Proverbs 31 woman. She sacrifices so much for others, especially for the children. And I have the security of knowing that things will go well at home. ✪

Kim's saving grace is her sense of humor.

Any wisdom about how you manage your military responsibilities, your family communications, and your spiritual life during deployments? Perhaps a piece of advice you can offer?

Dan: First of all, do not feel guilty for compartmentalizing different areas of your life. It is best to be focused on the mission at hand and do your utmost to accomplish every mission and take care of the troops under your care. A failure in either one of those, due to your lack of attention, will plague you personally for the rest of your life. I think it is okay for a man to place his family in the back of his mind for short periods of time to be able to focus on his job. This must be balanced with sensitivity to your wife's needs. You should not break predetermined expectations. If you realize something was an unrealistic expectation, talk about it again.

The one thing that we must not compartmentalize is our faithful walk with God. When we read the Psalms, we will find that God is close in safety and closer still in trouble. He knows all about war and is able to influence battle in accordance with His will. I found a bunch of verses to pray to the Lord when in contact with the enemy. I read in 2 Thessalonians 3:3, "The Lord is faithful. He will strengthen and protect you from the evil one." This was my constant prayer for the safety of those in my company.

If you realize something was an unrealistic expectation, talk about it again.

Matt: Use your non-deployed time to get built up spiritually. Once you are deployed you will most likely maintain what you've begun. Watch out for time-drainers like TV, movies, and video games. They are easy to turn to in your "down time" especially when you're stressed. Go to chapel. Pray. Seek out a Christian friend. ▶▶▶

Tim: We make most of it up as we go along. No really, I'm sure there is some of that, but mostly I ask the Lord, "Give me this day my daily bread." As I wake, I thank the Lord that I have life and breath today. Tomorrow is not promised to me, yet I have today to glorify God and enjoy Him forever.

Often I plan what I'm going to do when I get home. In my hometown there's a boardwalk that runs down the beach. Running along the "boards," with the salt air filling my nostrils and the ocean waves churning in the background, is also on my "to do" list when I return. And now that my children are old enough to ride their bikes next to daddy while he runs, they too experience the freedoms of America. The weather overseas during October is far from the fall days of most of the United States where the deep reds, oranges, and yellows sharpen the countryside. I can hardly wait to walk through an autumn forest and help my little ones gather a collage of God's handiwork. Hiking through the woods and exercising next to the ocean are things most Americans take for granted. Everyone can do these things when they want and they don't have to fear for their lives. Those thoughts keep me going, knowing that I have assumed the watch for now, but will be relieved by another Marine so that I can run the boardwalk, soak in the palate of fall colors, and enjoy so many other pursuits of life, liberty, and happiness. ✪

Daddy's Letter to Son

by LTC Frank Gray, USA

"The weapons we fight with are not the weapons of the world. On the contrary, they have divine power to demolish strongholds. We demolish arguments and every pretension that sets itself up against the knowledge of God, and we take captive every thought to make it obedient to Christ."

—2 Corinthians 10:4-5

Dear Son,

This is the first letter I have written to you in time of war. Unfortunately, there will be more. In this letter I will try to explain why your dad is back in the Army after the terrorist attacks on 9/11. Finally, I am asking you to pray for me because my one desire is to do my duty to my country, come home, and live my life in peace.

Son, there are evil people in this world, and they are set upon destroying our God, our nation, and our homes. They hate us simply for being Christians and Americans. This has been proven time and again by the attacks and planned violence on our way of life. The people who are doing this are terrorists, and they are our enemy. These terrorists must be destroyed if we are to live our lives with the freedom to worship our God and to keep our traditions as Americans.

It has been my prayer since 9/11 that my generation could fight these terrorists and defeat them. This is not to be so. My Special Forces comrades and I are on patrol every day throughout the world to secure our democracy and our freedoms. But we realize that it will take more than we can do in a lifetime.

Please know that your father—like Joshua, Caleb, and David—was hard-wired by God to be a soldier. I will spend the rest of my life defending our God, this nation, and our homes. You, too, must accept this responsibility. This does not mean you must grow up to be a soldier. But this does mean you must grow up to be a citizen of two kingdoms—God's and America. It is a sad day in a soldier's life when he must ask the next generation to pick up the gauntlet and be ready to defend our way of life. But in reading the Bible and history, I am not the first father to do so, nor will I be the last. ▶▶▶

Therefore, my son, you must grow up strong and smart, and be ready to fight. This is why your mother and I have insisted that you study hard and go to church every Sunday. This is also why we spend time every day teaching you our values, how to be a moral person, how to live a good life, and to love others. But it is up to you to learn these lessons. And it is also up to you to live a life worth living—a life given to the noble legacy of defending our God, our nation, and our homes.

Love always,
Daddy

Therefore, my son, you must grow up strong and smart, and be ready to fight.

The Sacrifice for Rebirth in Iraq

by *Capt Rob James, USMC*

It is the day before Easter, and a new chapter is about to begin in the lives of sixty-nine Iraqi men. That new chapter will put them and their families in great danger.

I attended the graduation this morning for these Iraqi police officers. One was twenty-years-old, and it was inspiring to see someone that young so willing to take on the great risk to make Iraq a country free from the lawlessness and instability it has endured for so many years.

I witnessed the pride on their faces as they rose from their plastic chairs in an unassuming tent to receive certificates signifying their success. These men sat quietly and respectfully at attention as the speaker recalled how over two hundred years ago, "a free America was formed amid the chaos of war." He told them how he, as a child, listened to stories about the brave men who risked their lives fighting for America's freedom.

He told the new policemen, "In the future, young Iraqi children will also hear stories about the brave men who fought for their freedom. You are those men."

To say these men are brave is, if anything, an understatement. But in the words of one of the graduates, "We understand many Iraqi policemen are getting killed, but we are here to help stabilize our country. It is our responsibility to protect Iraq and it is the responsibility of everyone who is making our region unstable to quit what they are doing and protect our nation."

Tomorrow, I will rise early and make my way to an Easter sunrise service with other Marines, Soldiers, Airmen, and Sailors. I will carry a weapon and be in body armor. As I go, I will think of my family and wonder what my wife and daughter are doing this Easter. I will also think of the men I was with this morning.

As I enjoy the fellowship and beauty of an Easter sunrise in Iraq, and remember the sacrifice my God made to guarantee me the true freedom and inner peace I enjoy, I will wonder where these men are. And as I thank God for the sacrifice His Son made for someone as insignificant as me, I will pray for the safety of these sixty-nine men, and I will pray for their courage as ▶▶▶

they face the tough road ahead. The road they have to travel will demand sacrifice, and some may pay with their lives.

I miss my family terribly, but am honored and humbled to be here and proud to do my part in making this a country whose children will some day enjoy the same peace, comfort, and safety as my own family does today. ✪

In the future, young Iraqi children will also hear stories about the brave men who fought for their freedom. You are those men.

Photo Courtesy of U.S. Army // by Air Force Master Sgt. Steve Cline

I Have Met Some Great Heroes

by CPT Kristine M. Varga, USA

I am an Army Nurse Corps Officer, currently deployed to Iraq with a combat support hospital. I work in the emergency room as a nurse, taking care of U.S. soldiers, Department of Defense civilians, and Iraqi soldiers and civilians; and in the sick call as a nurse practitioner, seeing everything from gastroenteritis to ankle sprains. I also play a pivotal role as a flight nurse, transporting patients when our hospital cannot meet the immediate needs of the patients due to limitations of equipment or manpower. Each role I play is a challenge and also a new experience. Each day I learn something new in medicine or something new about myself, from my strengths to my weaknesses as a nurse and also as a person. There is never a dull moment here.

It is hard to predict what each day holds. It is feast or famine. Some days can be very boring, with very few patients. Some days we get more than five casualties at one time. I honestly can say that there is no such thing as a "typical" day. Being here for almost six months, I have seen a unit come together as a family. The road was rough at first with adapting to our surroundings, getting used to the mortars, and learning to work together as a team.

We have had many close calls with mortars hitting our compound since we arrived. We could have sustained massive damage to our facility and also have had numerous casualties. But due to the mortar and rockets not detonating all the way or not detonating at all, we have managed to have minimal tragedy. I believe that God is present with us and He is watching over our safety. I, along with many other members of the hospital staff, have become much closer to God and have turned to Him for strength and courage.

I feel privileged to be a nurse and be one of the first persons to take care of patients who come through our doors. I have met some great heroes and will never forget the faces of the ones who have given the ultimate sacrifice. I have held soldiers' hands as they watched their buddies die, cried with patients when they found out they were never going to walk again, and offered my shoulder many times for soldiers to cry on. By being here, I have come to appreciate all that being a nurse stands for. We are able to make a difference in someone's life, be someone's hero for a day. ▶▶▶

Maybe one day there will be a memorial for all who served here. But for now, the best reward is seeing my patients leave here alive. A simple "thank you" is enough to keep me going in this stressful environment. It is a gift and a calling to be a nurse. We are the angels of mercy, the ones who comfort the sick and hurt. I feel blessed to have this calling upon my life. ✪

I have met some great heroes
and will never forget
the faces of the ones
who have given the
ultimate sacrifice.

Ordinary People Doing Extraordinary Things

by LTC Dave Segulin, USA

I have been meaning to write for some time about what goes on here. Most of what goes on is classified, so it makes it a tad difficult. But I wanted you to know some of the things that have been happening here with me and my boys.

First of all, know that there is progress every day. It may be small, even baby steps, but there is forward momentum. There are Iraqis here who stand up to violence and put themselves and their families at risk to ensure there is a future here for their children. Of course, things won't change overnight. Alongside these brave people are some of your ordinary American boys and girls who get up every day and do their duty.

A few days ago I was talking to a soldier who was feeling depressed. He asked me the secret for maintaining my high morale. I broke it down like this:

1) I have my faith and I am in the right place doing what the Lord has called me to do.

2) I pray and try to read the Bible every day.

3) I keep in contact with my wife and try to write daily.

4) When I need a boost I think of our very own "NASCAR pit crew."

The story of our "NASCAR pit crew" goes back to when we first arrived here. It was late at night and one of our vehicles hit a roadside bomb. It was the first one of our vehicles to hit one and everyone was in a flurry trying to figure out what had happened and what they needed to do to help out.

We brought the truck back to our base and the mechanics immediately went to work fixing our vehicle. These guys were a sight to see! Under the moonlight they descended on this vehicle in the spirit of a seasoned "NASCAR pit crew." They changed all the tires and repaired the vehicle so it was ready to roll back out.

I talked to my senior maintenance technician and he told me, "Yes, sir, we put a green door on (the truck was tan) so they (the terrorists) would know that they failed to keep this vehicle off the road."

While the pit crew worked on the truck, the medics worked on the vehicle's crew. Each man was checked out and returned to duty. As I said, this was our first incident. So no one would have begrudged these soldiers ▶▶▶

if they counted their blessings and called it a night. But they decided to send a message of their own to the terrorists. "We will not go quietly into the night. And we won't let terrorists win."

So when their truck was fixed with the green door, they climbed back in and headed back out on patrol. These guys inspired me. And, like I said, when I need a boost, I think of the time that we did not go quietly into the night.

Each day there are more stories like these of ordinary people doing extraordinary things. I am both honored and humbled to serve with them.

I just thought you should know some of what it's like to be here.

Thanks for all your support of us over here. But please remember to thank and pray for our loved ones that we left behind. In many ways I truly believe that they have it harder than we do. ✪

Each day there are more stories like these of ordinary people doing extraordinary things.

Photo Courtesy of OCF

Shepherd of Warriors

by CH(CPT) Don Williamson, USA

"I have fought the good fight, I have finished the race, I have kept the faith."
2 Timothy 4:7

I read that verse this past Sunday in chapel in praise to the Lord for getting us through this deployment. Yesterday, the last of the soldiers arrived back home. As I shared in chapel, our battalion miraculously suffered no fatalities or battlefield injuries. And there were countless times when there could have been many. The only explanation for this, of course, is God's grace and answered prayers. I cannot express my gratitude enough for how much your prayers and support have meant to me—and to all of our soldiers over these past fifteen months. You have blessed us more than you could ever know, and for that I say, "Thank you."

As I looked over the sea of people in the gym yesterday—soldiers hugging their family members with cameras rolling to catch every precious moment—I was struck by the reminder that even though this battle is over, the war is not—neither the war on terror nor the war for people's souls. While we may experience peace for a season, I'm reminded that there will be no lasting peace until the Prince of Peace returns. So until then, I will continue to run to the battle, wherever that takes me. The calling to be a chaplain—the shepherd of warriors—is indeed an honor.

A couple of nights ago, I was putting my younger two daughters to bed. After telling them a story, and praying with them, I gave them each a kiss goodnight and rejoiced at being able to tell them I would see them in the morning. As I turned out the light and got ready to leave, my daughter stopped me in the doorway.

"Daddy," she asked, "Are you a hero?"

I turned around to face her. "No, baby. I'm just a chaplain," I smiled in reply with tears welling up in my eyes. "But God allowed me to minister to a whole battalion of heroes."

With that, I closed the door to their room—and to one of the greatest years of ministry I've ever had the privilege to experience. ✪

Front Line Quotes

"It was crazy, the emotions going through my body as we rode back [from an ambush]. I wanted to kill everyone I saw, out of fear. And then I was also thinking I should wave at everyone like normal so they would think everything was fine and we were invincible! I started singing to God as we rode and I looked into the peoples' eyes (so many filled with hate) knowing that they couldn't touch me, not a hair on my body, unless the God of the Angel Armies allowed them to. And to tell you the truth, anything an Almighty God wants is going to be just fine with me, because He is good, He loves me, and I trust Him."

—Cpl Josh Wicker, USMC

"I've had my highs and lows spiritually. I thought that being in a combat zone would be one of those highs—helping build my relationship with God. But I haven't found that to be the case. Combat brings into reality the fragility of life, and I've experienced it firsthand with the death of one of my own soldiers. But as a leader, it also brings new stresses like making snap life-or-death decisions concerning the safety of my men. These can be consuming, not leaving as much time for the 'God factor' as I would like.

What I've learned is that loving God is neither easier nor harder when you're amidst stressful, dangerous situations. Regardless of my circumstances, I must daily, consciously 'Seek first the kingdom of God' and He promises to help with the rest (Matthew 6:33). Proverbs 3:5-6 says to 'Trust in the Lord with all your heart and lean not on your own understanding; in all your ways acknowledge Him, and He will make your paths straight.' I'm learning that I need to worry less and trust God more because He is ultimately in control and can do a much better job of providing safety than I can, anyway."

—CPT Jim Freeze, USA

"There is not a single soldier I have talked to who plans on making Iraq, or their trailer, or their tent, their permanent place of residence. We identify ourselves as strangers in this land, and it is in this environment where God has shown me how we should view our lives here on earth—from the perspective of a stranger. This seems to fly in the face of conventional wisdom. We all desire a place to call home, a place to relax, to find comfort. God desires the same thing for us. But the problem occurs when we choose to make this earth our home, and seek to fulfill our deepest longings and desires with empty, non-eternal substitutes.

First Peter is written to "strangers in this world," stressing the imperishable aspects of our faith and contrasting them with the temporal idols of this world. Peter repeats—in fact, begs—for us to remember we are strangers and aliens here. This deployment has shown me what it looks like to live as a stranger on earth. No one has to point out that Iraq is not my home: I am reminded of that fact every second of every day. God has taught me that when I am out of my comfort zone—when I am truly a stranger to the environment around me—then He has my attention.

The real question, then, is, "Will heaven still be on my mind when I am back in the States?" I have decided that although Iraq is a unique country, I have no desire to stay. I long to go home. In the same way, we must fix our minds on Jesus Christ and spending eternity with Him. It's easy—through the eyes of a stranger—to see how we are supposed to live our lives."

—1LT T.J. Menn, USA ✪

SCRIPTURES

Psalm 31:21
Praise be to the Lord, for he showed his wonderful love to me when I was in a besieged city.

Psalm 40:2
He lifted me out of the slimy pit, out of the mud and mire; he set my feet on a rock and gave me a firm place to stand.

Psalm 61:2
From the ends of the earth I call to you, I call as my heart grows faint; lead me to the rock that is higher than I.

Psalm 91:1-2
He who dwells in the shelter of the Most High will rest in the shadow of the Almighty. I will say of the Lord, "He is my refuge and my fortress, my God, in whom I trust."

1 Corinthians 10:13
No temptation has seized you except what is common to man. And God is faithful; he will not let you be tempted beyond what you can bear. But when you are tempted, he will also provide a way out so that you can stand up under it.

1 Corinthians 15:57-58
But thanks be to God! He gives us the victory through our Lord Jesus Christ. Therefore, my dear brothers, stand firm. Let nothing move you. Always give yourselves fully to the work of the Lord, because you know that your labor in the Lord is not in vain.

Titus 2:6
Similarly, encourage the young men to be self-controlled.

James 4:7
Submit yourselves, then, to God. Resist the devil, and he will flee from you.

ON THE HOME FRONT

Apart or A Part?

During deployment, how do you keep your spouse ever present in the children's minds?

Joanna: Web cams are great! Our 12-month-old could play "Peek-a-boo" (though there was a bit of a delay) over the computer, and the older kids could play "Simon Says." They did get to talk to their dad on the phone some, but mostly they drew him pictures. He wrote a story for them, sending a page at a time so they'd have something to anticipate from dad. We tried to send a package about twice a month with cookies or something they could help make for him.

Kim: I talk about their daddy a lot. When I'm cuddling the kids, I remind them how much daddy loves and misses them. If we're doing something he would like to do, we talk about how much fun he'd have with us. We often take pictures of whatever we are doing to send to him.

Meredith: We took lots of pictures of Matt with each child before he left. Then I put together a "Daddy and Me" photo album for each child. It was full of pictures of him doing things with us, loving us, and being a part of our lives, so it reminded them of our life together.

We also hung family pictures all over the stairwell, pictures of us all together, pictures of each one with dad and pictures of grandparents and special family friends. Every day as we walked up and down those stairs, it was a great chance to remind ourselves of dad and of all the people who love us and are praying for us. It reminded me of the great cloud of witnesses that are surrounding us, cheering us to run with perseverance the race marked out for us. ▶▶▶

Similarly, I tried to bring him into almost everything we did by telling stories about him, or adding his comments to our discussions. I reminded them that dad likes coffee when we walked down that aisle at the commissary. I reminded them that he had given them special gifts because he loves them. I also made sure they knew that daddy was obeying God by doing his job well and taking good care of his soldiers—and that we had an important job to take care of the families of daddy's soldiers. I wanted them to know that the sacrifices they were making were for a purpose. I tried to share with them the vision that this was our chance to serve God. ✪

They did get to talk to their dad on the phone some, but mostly they drew him pictures.

"I Want My Daddy!"

How do you respond to children when they cry or get angry about dad being gone?

Joanna: One of our daughters was my barometer. I could tell we were doing too much or I wasn't taking enough individual time with her because she would have a meltdown and start with the "I miss daddy" routine. (Of course, they always seemed to want daddy when it was discipline time.) But I was careful to say, "I miss him a lot, too," or "I understand how you feel because God made a family to have a mommy and a daddy. But you know he is doing what God has called him to do right now, and we have to pray that God will keep him safe." I made a point *not* to say, "He'll be home soon" or "God will bring him back soon" because you just never know what might happen. I didn't want them to think that God was not answering their prayers or be bitter at God (or me!) if daddy didn't come home.

When there was a meltdown, I tried to slow down a bit and relax our schedule—maybe take the children out for ice cream or a family fun night. I'd try to do something fun to take their minds off the fact that he was gone and show them, instead, that we could still have a fun time as a family.

Kim: When my kids share their feelings of being sad because daddy's gone, I confess that I feel the same way. We share a lot of the same feelings. We talk about what we miss most about him or what we're going to do as soon as we see him again. I like to try to get them talking about something fun we all did with daddy or a special time they had together. We usually end up laughing over a funny story that included him.

Meredith: When they told me they were sad or they missed daddy, I would enter into it with them. I'd assure them that I really missed him, too. I would hold them and just be with them for a while. Then we would move on, either by talking about what he might be doing now or what we needed to be doing, or just encouraging them to go to sleep so they would be ready for the next day. ✪

Discipline Issues

What are some ways you maintained order and/or disciplined your children? Do you have advice or lessons learned?

Joanna: I made a chart of family rules along with morning and evening charts so the kids would know what was expected of them each morning and at bedtime. I laminated the charts, and we went over them together. It helped us pull together as a family, and it saved a lot of repetitive discussions as we went through our days.

Meredith: I didn't want their dad's absence to be an excuse for bad behavior, but I didn't want them not to be able to express their feelings, either. There were times I felt at a loss in discipline. I found that when I prayed about it, the Lord was really faithful to show me what to do. When our son started misbehaving, I thought I needed to spank him more often. That made him more angry. As I prayed about it, the Lord showed me that our son's love language was touch, and he wasn't getting enough from me. When I used touch to discipline him, it was hurtful. God showed me that I needed to hold him more, and use other forms of correction when necessary. The result was amazing.

Another friend shared with me the value of considering the way their dad shows the children love and encouraged me to meet some of their needs that way. Dad's absence leaves a void they are used to having filled. You can't be both mom and dad, but you can try to show love in different ways. ✪

God showed me that I needed to hold him more.

Let's Take a Trip

Do you go on trips/vacations while your spouse is away?

Kim: We've had a great time on our trips while Tim was away. In the summer of one deployment we went to a wedding in South Carolina, home to New Jersey, and we visited a friend in Florida who rented a house for the summer. The kids had so much fun on our trips and made great memories. We wanted daddy to feel like he was a part of it, so we made sure to tell him all about it and took lots of pictures. Even the little ones can draw pictures of their favorite parts of the trip and the older ones can write letters and notes or e-mails. Sure, it takes some planning and work, but it's well worth it for making memories.

Joanna: We planned enough big and little trips to keep us looking forward to something each month. It might be traveling for a weekend visit to a friend close by or a month-long excursion across the country, but we planned and enjoyed adventures along the way. It was definitely a time of refreshment, and it often provided me with some wonderful adult company and extra helping hands.

Meredith: Schedules and organization are crucial in keeping a family sane, but excursions and breaks are just as important—and lots of fun! We got out the calendar and made great plans for trips and outings, so we always knew there was something around the corner. Then after the excitement we were glad to get back to normal. We received a lot of support from friends and family. Both sets of our parents, our siblings, and various friends came to visit. We decided that we were making extra money and we were willing to spend it on what would be encouraging to us, even if it meant flying out a family member or a friend for a weekend. This was helpful for me because I knew there would be a time when I would have another adult around to help me with a task or to watch the kids while I worked on a big project. ✪

Handling Home Front Holidays
How Deployments Affect the Holidays
by Sarah Arnett, Army wife, Tennessee and Sarah Curry, Army wife, Georgia

When spouses are deployed over Thanksgiving and Christmas, an additional challenge is presented to home front families. How closely will we stick to our traditions? Do I even feel like "doing" the holidays this year? Thanks be to God that Thanksgiving and Christmas can both still hold their joy for spouses, children, and the deployed soldiers, too. Can it be just the same as if they were home? No. Can it be joyful? With God's help, yes.

As families who have faced this holiday scenario, here are a few lessons we learned:

1. Pray, pray, pray. Pray that the Lord will sustain you and that your heart will be drawn to your Savior and your spouse in a new way. Pray for all of the deployed service men and women, and for their families. Search the Scriptures and claim God's promises for your children, your spouse, and yourself.

2. Be realistic about what you can do. A perfectly planned and executed holiday does not automatically make it a happy one. Do your best to make it special, but don't think that doing more will make it better. If you are a home front spouse this year, decide what is most important to you and just do your best.

3. Determine in advance to keep a positive outlook. Many well-intentioned souls (often including our own families) become especially "sorry for you" during the holidays. It is okay to publicly acknowledge that you would rather have your deployed loved one home, but it is also okay to truly enjoy the season. Honestly tell others that while you appreciate their concern, you have decided to focus on your blessings and the joy of Lord.

4. Remember the reason for Christmas. It is the same this year as it ever was—Jesus was born a baby so that we could be His children. This foundation stands true whether you carry out your traditions or make new ones. When your celebrations center around Christ, others will notice. What an opportunity to share the reason for the hope that is in us (1 Peter 3:15)!

Celebrating the holidays without your spouse is hard. To your children, though, it signals that the reason for our joy doesn't change with circumstances. During the holiday season, cling to Jesus. He is our unchanging strength. ✪

Deployed...Again

by Jacquline Grose, Army wife, Midwest

When our soldiers train for deployment, they do not sit back and wonder when an attack will come: they anticipate the attack. They do not sustain an attack and then take defeat without an effort to defend: they defend themselves and counterattack. They do not take defeat and then feel bad and unable to do better on the next attack; they regroup, reassess, and plan to fight again, having learned from the experience. Our soldiers use military intelligence to anticipate when an attack may come. They plan how to respond to an assault so as to be victorious. They train their bodies and minds to be vigilant and brave.

As the wife of a soldier, I have a similar calling on the home front. My attacks don't come in the form of men with rifles or IEDs. Home front attacks are temptations to be lonely, fearful, depressed, or overwhelmed.

When Chris and I married, we agreed that the military is a mission field for Christians, and we could see many ways that we could serve and reach out as a Christian military family. Even so, it was hard when our first deployment came. I was very consumed with the idea that I would have to "do all of this" by myself. I was lonely, bitter, and resentful.

When the deployment was over, I felt that I had just barely survived. I was sure that God had carried my weak and weary self through it, but there was no joy or victory.

When deployment number two came along, I already knew that I wasn't good at this separation thing. I felt robbed, angry, and ripped apart. That wound remained raw for the duration of the deployment. I was volatile in dealing with difficulties at home. Though I had lots of loving church members who supported me and were an extension of God's love, my outlook was still gloomy.

I lived only for Chris's return, and had very little joy or peace. But I knew there had to be a better way to go through deployment, and I hoped God would show me soon because I knew there would be at least one more deployment.

I felt God showing me that there could be a deployment that was not consumed with coping and waiting and pining and resenting. Life during deployment could be purposeful, and a time when joy and peace would reign.

As I studied God's Word, a new motivation sprang up inside me. Colossians 3:12-14 talks about putting on compassion, forgiveness, and love. Ephesians 6:10-18 talks about putting on the full armor of God. Philippians 4:8 tells us to think about the things that are true, noble, pure, lovely, and excellent. None of these things have a caveat that says, "If you *feel* like loving, love" or "If you *feel* strong enough, put on the full armor of God" or, "If you *feel* like disciplining your mind to focus on the good things, then do it." The verses are commands to *do* those things—with a reminder that peace will follow. I think this is the element that I had been missing.

During the first two deployments, though I had been praying, studying God's Word, and surrounding myself with encouraging believers, I let my emotions rule the day. I routinely responded to difficulty with great emotion and little acknowledgement that God is in control and ordains life's events for good. This is much too tiring when God has abundant life available to me. Furthermore, my five children will copy the behavior and attitudes I model for them.

God was preparing me to be a wise soldier, learning from my mistakes and anticipating the enemy's attack. I was learning to be slow to anger and abounding in love, not to become defeated as the adversary would like, but to deal with challenges in a way that aligns with Jesus' teachings. I still wondered if my husband and I could be victorious, peaceful, and joyful even ▶▶▶

As I studied God's Word, a new motivation sprang up inside me.

when we were half a world apart. I wondered if my children could miss their daddy but still continue to grow up and have peace, letting go of anger in a healthy way. I wondered if Chris could communicate his spiritual influence from the other side of the world.

Now that we are into deployment number three, I can say, "Yes!" to most of these things. I am excited about how God is intervening during this deployment—excited not to be needy and depressed. I don't want to barely survive: I want life to be abundant even while we live separately, joined by long distance communication. I have accepted the peace God gives.

During this deployment I am focusing on questions like: *How can God be glorified through this deployment? How can I be a supportive wife for my husband? How will God fill in the gaps when I am not up to the task?* and *How can I serve others and make their experience better?*

We learned recently that there will be a three-month extension to the original year-long deployment. While I am not excited about this, I am not going to allow my whole life to fall apart because of changing circumstances. God is able to hold us up joyfully for twelve months, and He can sustain us joyfully for three more. It's not difficult for Him. ✪

I don't want to barely survive: I want life to be abundant.

Hope for the Home Front

by Marshéle Carter Waddell, Navy wife, Colorado

"Mommy, what is a pirate?" asked Jenna, a kindergartner at the time.

"Well, Honey," I replied, "a pirate is someone who takes over the ships of other people."

"Mommy, is *daddy* a pirate?"

Her fresh insight caught me off guard. At five-years-old her perspective of her dad's job responsibilities was amazingly accurate. Although Mark doesn't wear the black eye patch and the gold earring—and yes, he still has all his teeth—my youngest's understanding of her father's career captured my attention.

I am convinced that life as a "military brat" yields a unique worldview. My young children must have thought Uncle Sam was a distant relative, the all-powerful patriarch who shaped every aspect of our family life. *Quarters* weren't just coins, but home. The *exchange* wasn't a fair trade but the store where they got everything from pencils to pants. Going to the doctor meant meeting yet another stranger because the medical staff transferred as often as we did. Daddy's office wasn't a building, but a ship, a sub, an airplane, a Quonset hut, or a firing range. Dad disappeared into vacuous, black holes every morning and, on occasion, reappeared after sunset. Other times, the days ran together, becoming weeks and months, and daddy didn't reappear. Their dad's commute was also atypical. He arrived home on bikes, ferries, aircraft carriers, and kayaks.

When we browse family photo albums, I determine which baby is in the picture by the clues in the background. There's a dormitory, university kiosks, and red-and-gold sweatshirts; that must be baby Josh at Arizona State University where Mark used his VEAP benefits to attend college. There's white sand, golden sunshine, turquoise tide, and submarines; that must be baby Jordan in Hawaii. And there's pine and oak trees towering over salmon-colored impatiens and azaleas in the front yard; that must be baby Jenna in Virginia. The photos reveal a sobering fact: most Easters, Christmases and birthdays are celebrated *sans* dad. The picture feels off balance, teetering with only one parent in the frame, or more often, no parent at all because the only parent present is taking the picture. ▶▶▶

Walk Beside Me and Be My Friend

Josh, three-years-old, and I, pregnant with a second child, rode with Mark to the pier that rainy morning. Our painful goodbyes had been stretched over several days, prolonged by a necessary delay to repair the submarine. We were all emotionally numb. Yet more tears found their way to our swollen eyes as we savored one last family embrace.

Josh and I sat silently in the car watching the sub's hatch swallow Mark. We wouldn't hear a word from him for months. We wouldn't see him again for half a year.

"I don't want daddy to work *anymore!*" Josh declared, pushing his lower lip as far out as it would go and crossing his arms with a hmmph!

I patiently tried to explain, "If daddy didn't work, we wouldn't have a home or food or even a car."

"Then we'll just have to *walk!*" he firmly concluded. It was that simple to him. At least, he reasoned, with no home, no food, and no car, he'd be walking beside his dad.

I think our daughter Jordan's first complete sentence was, "Where's daddy?" She asked me this question at least twenty-five times a day for months at a time. My answer was always the same, "At work, honey."

"But, *whyyyyyy*, mommy? Where *is* he?!" Answers didn't come easily; partly because of her tender age, she couldn't have understood the whole story. The truth was even *I* didn't know the whys and wheres or the how longs.

Independence Day

The military family usually consists of one active duty person and the dependents. That's us, the dependents: a dependent wife and three dependent progeny. Ironically, *in*dependence is demanded of us *de*pendents. Every time daddy laces up his spit-shined, black combat boots and weighs anchor, mommy must now fill two pairs of shoes, his and hers, as his walk away.

Fulfilling the mom/dad role taps and exhausts my every resource. Four arms for consoling little bruised knees and small broken hearts are instantly reduced to two. Two resourceful souls and two minds filled with timely answers for a child's perplexing questions diminish to one. One of the two storehouses of energy and creativity must suddenly supply the demand alone, doubly depleted and doubly drained.

Weeks and months of this can leave a mother frazzled and fatigued. At times, I would pay anyone any amount just to answer the next kid-question or meet the next kid-need. General Norman Schwartzkopf said it right when speaking of his mother in his book, *It Doesn't Take a Hero*, "I think mom would have been glad if she could have gone off to war, too....Instead, she found herself in tedious, completely unheroic circumstances on the home front....She found herself a single mother with a large house, three kids, and a way of life that was impossible to sustain on Army pay."

When Boys Are the Men of the House

"We're the *men* of the house," three-year-old Josh announced at dinner on an evening when Mark was home. As they congratulated each other on their greatness of gender, we all shared a good laugh.

It is true, three-year-old boys are little men in the making. It pains me deeply though to hear departing dads say to their young sons, "You're the man of the house now. Take good care of your mother and your brothers ▶▶▶

> It is true, three-year-old boys are little men in the making.

and sisters. I'm counting on you." How ill-timed and unfair this is in my experience and opinion. Little boys are little boys. Their shoulders are not large enough or strong enough for carrying a burden that heavy. We have made a conscious effort never to say or imply that to our son. With each deployment, we have tried to give him the freedom to be and to enjoy his age, and to take on only those responsibilities appropriate to his maturity.

Likewise, while Mark is underway, I have been careful not to rely on my son, and now on his sisters, as my confidantes. Children of any age don't deserve the weight of adult fears and concerns being dumped into their laps, and it is not rational or reasonable to look for or expect adult counsel or comfort from a child. It is our role to listen to the child's fears and concerns, not visa versa, no matter how desperate or lonely or frightened we may feel.

A Father to the Fatherless

During fatherless times, babysitters and family members and friends are helpful, but none enable and replenish me like my Heavenly Father. I run to *Him*, relax in *His* arms, and draw on *His* strength daily as I am forced to be both mom and dad. He reminds me to teach my children that only one Father is constant, ever present, and all-powerful. I fall to my knees at the end of many days and through tears praise Him that, because of His promises, even a seemingly fatherless childhood will work for each child's good and to His glory. God's word comforts me. "He defends the cause of the fatherless," and "A father to the fatherless, a defender of widows, is God in his holy dwelling" (Deuteronomy 10:18, Psalm 68:5).

Alone, I don't have the 24/7 stamina which is a prerequisite of a mother on double duty. Neither do my children have endless inner strength to live without a dad most of their growing up years. Nor do I have all the answers to their whys, wheres and hows.

God promises that "those who hope in the Lord will renew their strength. They will soar on wings like eagles; they will run and not grow weary, they will walk and not be faint" (Isaiah 40:31). That's one potent prescription for "single" parents and "fatherless" kids because both circumstances require so much walking with endurance, running with courage, and soaring with faith over difficult circumstances. All these are ours for the asking, leatherbound atop our nightstands. ✪

God's Children
The Daily Sacrifices of Military Children
by Eileen K. Fant, Air Force wife, Hawaii

I live with four remarkable people. Each day, I watch in awe as they wake up, do their schoolwork, eat, and sleep. If you looked, you would see four ordinary looking children. But when I look, I see heroes.

What makes them heroes is not their parents or grandparents or accomplishments. It is simply the life that God has called them to live: the lives of military children.

I often read stirring accounts of those who face danger every day in the defense of our country. I read praises of their spouses. It is time to acknowledge the youngest and bravest warriors among us, our children. They have each been chosen by God for their role in our families, and the lessons I have learned as their mother are innumerable. ▶▶▶

It is time to acknowledge the youngest and bravest warriors among us, our children.

Trust

Two days before our oldest son, David's third birthday, my husband, Bob, and I knelt beside his bed. We struggled for the words to explain why his world would be completely transformed in the next ten hours. His birthday party would not happen. Bob would not see him blow out the candles on the birthday cake. The next morning David, our infant son Jonathan, and I would board an evacuation flight. We would leave the only home David knew, in the Middle East. Bob tried to explain, but it was David who defined the truth: "If it isn't safe for us, why is Daddy staying?" When we explained it was Bob's job to stay, David listened carefully. We ended our talk with prayer, and David snuggled down in his bed, trusting that we would take care of him. The next day he held tight to my hand as we walked to the plane that took us away from our home, leaving his father behind. His childlike trust gave me courage.

David's trust in us painted a clear picture of the trust I need to have in my heavenly Father. Matthew 6:26-27 says, "Look at the birds of the air; they do not sow or reap or store away in barns, and yet your heavenly Father feeds them. Are you not much more valuable than they? Who of you by worrying can add a single hour to his life?"

Sacrifice

The call shocked all of us. Out of the blue Bob was asked whether he would be willing to deploy. He called me. The three hours allotted for a decision drove us to our knees. I gathered our children and prayed. I struggled to explain what this separation would mean. It meant daddy would miss two birthdays and Easter. It meant daddy would not be there to teach Bible study each morning or eat dinner with us each evening. It would create a huge vacuum in our day-to-day lives.

It was easy to explain the reason Bob needed to go. I told them that with our military support children there could go to sleep at night without being afraid. Daddy needed to go so other daddies could kiss their children good night knowing they were safe. David and Jonathan were old enough to process the meaning. Both swallowed hard and said they thought he should go. They reasoned they could loan him out if other children would be blessed. Their willingness to give up their dad for others humbled me.

With our present world situation, even more military children are being asked to make this sacrifice. I am sure they will step up to the demand just as my children did. Military children make sacrifices so others can live in security.

In Philippians 2:4 Paul writes clearly what a military child learns at a young age, "Each of you should look not only to your own interests, but also to the interests of others." Our children have learned these lessons at a tender age. Yet while they have learned the tough lessons, they have also learned what it means to be abundantly blessed. Because our lives only make sense when viewed as God-ordered, they have seen the hand of God repeatedly upon their lives. They have faced scary situations, and have personally witnessed God meeting their needs in exciting and wonderful ways.

Through varying circumstances, they have had the unique opportunity of allowing God to mold and refine them. They have seen God answer the big prayers, and answer the ones only spoken in their hearts. They know God will meet them in the quiet places when things are tough. They know that God is a God who can be trusted because He has never left them, no matter where they are. They are heroes of faith, young warriors with a purpose. They are military kids. ✪

They are heroes of faith, young warriors with a purpose. They are military kids.

In the Presence of Heroes

by Cindy Brown, Army wife, Colorado Springs, Colorado

When it came time to choose a career path, many of my high school and college friends opted for careers in the medical field. Not me! Blood, pain, bodily fluids—UGH! My plans—all things easily accomplished in an air-conditioned office—were put on hold when I married a soldier.

So here I was, after tying the knot with my man in uniform, stationed in Germany while the love of my life commanded a brigade of military policemen in a war zone. Because an MP's existence is almost always "outside the wire," there were numerous daily opportunities for injury. Those whose injuries could be stabilized at the CASH (combat hospital) would be sent to Landstuhl Army Medical Center in Germany, often within twenty-four hours of their initial injury. Because our brigade families were already forward deployed in Germany, and headquartered only about an hour from Landstuhl hospital, my husband hoped that some of the wives might feel inclined to be a team of visitors to cheerlead our wounded soldiers. Not wanting to disappoint my husband, but not too sure I wanted to lead this visitation team, I asked for volunteers from our Family Readiness Group. There was very little response and most were more hesitant than myself. The general consensus was, "How can I do that when my husband is in the very same place where these warriors were injured?" These were exactly the same thoughts I'd had. Still, I wanted to set the example. But how could I when my heart, head—and stomach!—didn't know if I could?

My first thoughts were honestly to "allow" the rear detachment team to handle it alone. Wasn't it their job? Then the Holy Spirit pricked my hard heart, and asked in a very quiet but firm voice, "What if this was your husband? Your son? Wouldn't you want someone to visit and offer encouragement and hope in what could seem to be a very hopeless situation?"

"Well, yes, but...."

"But what?"

It was only by the strength of God and the commitment of the Spirit that I made that first visit—and never looked back.

At Landstuhl, I saw unimaginable things while talking with soldiers who had multiple burns, fractures, lacerations—injuries that no one outside of an emergency room should ever have to see. In and of myself, I am unable to tolerate those sights. But by God's grace, I looked directly into those maimed faces and saw past the injuries to their beautiful and hopeful spirits.

Every soldier I visited shared his hopes of life after his body healed. A soldier without feet dreamed of dancing at his brother's wedding. Others who had been blinded talked about rejoining their buddies and completing missions they had begun together. No self-pity. Never a "why me?" Only hope and determination. And I, who had tiptoed into the minefield of visiting the critically wounded, left the hospital after each visit, having been blessed to be in the presence of such heroes. ✪

I left the hospital after each visit, having been blessed to be in the presence of such heroes.

Chaplains and Deployment

by Susan Causey, Army Chaplain wife, Kansas

On a recent autumn afternoon, some friends and I sat around a table enjoying slices of warm pumpkin bread while we talked about our experiences—particularly with deployments—as wives of army soldiers who also have the privilege to serve as chaplains. The chaplaincy motto, "Pro Deo et Patria"—for God and Country—sums up the focus and direction of our lives as military families. These are two great callings and, as such, have unique demands and rewards.

When dealing with deployments, there is no "one" experience. There is no cookie cutter pattern that will define the command climate, the mission, the duration, the location, the people, the place in life, or any other aspect of a deployment. Just in our small group that afternoon we had one wife, Teresa, with a newly adopted baby, still in their first duty station but on their second deployment. There was another wife, Susan, with grown children, who had been in the military for awhile and yet, due to assignments and schooling, this was their first deployment. And for me, we've had multiple deployments over the twenty-two years we've been in the military. We each have our own stories. Life changes and so do deployments.

However, some things don't ever change, especially the needs of chaplains serving our soldiers and country in forward deployed positions. The biggest need is for prayer. Our chaplains are fighting battles on multiple fronts. There is the obvious physical front where the Army chaplain lives, eats, breathes, and ministers alongside the fighting soldiers. Chaplains are classified as non-combatants by the Geneva Convention and, therefore, do not carry weapons. Chaplains are sometimes seen as "good luck charms" by the soldiers who somewhat superstitiously stick close to the chaplain for protection—not realizing, but hopefully seeing and learning, that God loves them and cares for them. They are sometimes seen as morale officers, delivering ice cream sandwiches in the heat to boost spirits. They are often seen as the one to comfort and counsel in times of distress and grief. They are seen as religious officers to engage the national religious leaders. They are our soldiers who need our prayers and our encouragement. They are soldiers both for our country and for God. We need to pray for their physical safety and endurance.

On the emotional front, chaplains deal with the same soldier stresses: being away from home, dealing with extreme heat and cold, adrenaline surges as danger stalks their steps, and living in challenging conditions—all while trying to carry out a mission. Part of their job is the morale of their units as well as their spiritual health. In spite of the fatigue, they need to be positive and encouraging as they deal with many harsh, dark aspects of life and death in the lives of the soldiers around them. We need to pray for encouragement and endurance for their hearts and minds.

Finally, on a spiritual front, the chaplains are on the front line. They are opposing the powers of darkness, and Satan would like to make them ineffective or discredit their efforts. The depravity of man is clearly seen as our chaplains wade through the wreckage of the many lives they deal with. The need for God's grace and Christ's salvation is so evident. We must pray for their spiritual refreshment and for God's wisdom to guide them and His strength to sustain them.

On the home front, some things change and some remain constant. As spouses, we also have the opportunity to minister—to our families, the communities we are in, and our chaplain spouses. This takes on different forms and expressions as our lives, locations, and circumstances change. Sometimes it requires the home parent to "circle the wagons" and ▶▶▶

They are soldiers both for our country and for our God.

minister primarily in the home, to assure that the children are secure and dealing with the strains of having a parent deployed. Other times, there are opportunities for more ministry outside of the home, working with other spouses of deployed soldiers, supporting the command structure, community volunteer work, weekly prayer groups, unit Bible study, "chick-flick" nights, and monthly dinner/program events.

Ironically, one thing about a deployment that can be almost exciting is the opportunity for new avenues to minister, and to see what God has in store for us, as individuals, to do. Yet there are the lonely nights; the missed holidays, birthdays, anniversaries, and significant events; as well as the day-to-day sharing of life. These are the common elements shared by all military members and their families. It is a high price to pay. Yet we can pray that God will redeem the time in His economy for His eternal purposes. ✪

Lessons learned through deployments:

• Everyone benefits from the encouragement of spoken words and actions.

• God can use us as individuals to do things we never thought we could.

• God is the one constant, "an anchor for the soul, firm and secure" (Hebrews 6:19), to hold onto during the challenges of deployment.

Job and the Reserve Soldier's Wife

by Sue Faulk, Army Reserve wife, Michigan

As an Army Reserve soldier's wife, I empathize with Job.

Job's life is going well. He has a wonderful family, good friends, a comfortable living, and a rich faith life. Then the rug is pulled out from under him. My life is usually cruising along OK, too, until my husband gets deployed.

Job did everything well. So well, in fact, that God Himself was willing to bet that Job's faithfulness would not falter when the devil was so sure that it would. Can you imagine developing faith so strong God Himself would bet on you?

Job's friends couldn't believe that Job could or should be so faithful. Their discussion of God's seeming failure to support and protect Job is compelling. Neighbors and acquaintances have had the same types of reactions to my husband's adventures. "When will he be done playing soldier?" and "We shouldn't even be there!" and "How could he leave you?" are conversation starters or well-meant expressions of sympathy. That last one is especially disconcerting to me. The implication that my soldier, to fulfill an obligation or an oath, is willing to leave me on a whim, or that maybe he doesn't really love me, is annoying. There is temptation to weigh those thoughts in the wee, lonely hours during deployments.

No one can blame Job for railing at God. For questioning his purpose in life. For being just plain mad about what was happening to him. For feeling deeply the loss of his family. Still, Job enters into conversation with God. He knows God is there, listening to every word. He expects God to answer him, and doesn't turn away. And when God reminds Job that He is the one who filled the oceans, and separates darkness from light, and calls the sun to rise and set, Job isn't offended. He listens and gets the point: "The Lord gives, the Lord takes away. Blessed be the name of the Lord." *The man lost everything!* But he knows deep-down in his soul, he will not lose God—and God will not lose sight of him. Job offers praise even in the midst of personal chaos, stays close to God, and is rewarded in ways that only God rewards a faithful servant.

Following Job's example, talking to God even when I'm in a decidedly negative state of mind is vital to my deployment survival. I know I will be ▶▶▶

heard. "Why do I have to go to family events alone?" "Why do I have to go to school meetings as a single parent?" "What will I do if I answer the knock at the door and see a uniformed officer and a chaplain?" I have shared these experiences with others who have the same concerns, sometimes having conversations like the ones Job had with his friends, sometimes ranting a little at God, too. God is willing to listen to our gripes and to comfort us in our darkest hours. In three deployments, I haven't gotten direct, conversational answers from God like Job did. But I have made it through each deployment, and have been able to see and feel the good that these adventures have brought with them. Maybe that is the answer to a healthy soul during deployments: "Keep talking! Keep listening!"

During marriage preparation classes, one critical point was clear as my soldier and I got ready for this life-changing event: what we were about to do was not form a contract or an alliance, but create a covenant. The two of us and God were creating an indivisible bond for life. Making God a "full partner" in the equation was a necessary element. Because of this covenant, neither of us is truly alone though others might think we are. God is with me when my husband is away, and with my husband when I am far from him.

Our family looks like a lot of other families at first glance. We live like a lot of regular people in a neighborhood where people walk their dogs in the mornings and evenings, where kids ride bikes on the sidewalks and play ball on the lawns. I go to church, serve there in various capacities, support school activities, help with soccer and baseball—just like other moms do. We don't live on or near a post or base. I doubt most of our neighbors would even recognize my husband in uniform! But when the call to duty comes, my husband becomes a soldier. And my house and routines and school and church and family activities still go on—minus one adult. We may look like a lot of other families, even during deployments. But it's not the same.

Being a soldier is a calling, not a job or a career. Even though reservists only do their "soldier thing" on a part-time basis, the commitment is still the same and, in some ways, perhaps more challenging. They may be called on at any time to turn their plowshare into a sword, and are expected to complete the mission given them as 100 percent soldier. There isn't a note at the bottom of their orders that says they only have to do 10 percent of the job because they only spend "one weekend a month and two weeks a year" training. That slogan fails to mention weekly administration nights, evenings of conference calls, resident schools, or the requirement that his civilian employer is without a key employee for a while. To those they serve and serve with, they are soldiers. Not "soldiers with an asterisk."

It certainly is a calling of sorts for me, too, but rarely takes the form I thought it would. These adventures can bring chaos of mind and heart. Sometimes those who don't understand military families just believe everything is sailing along as usual, whether my husband is in-country or out of the country, at work, or at the Army.

We walk by faith, and not by sight. God gives us help to succeed and examples to follow at every turn, if we're willing to acknowledge His presence. I have to continue my conversation with God just as Job did, always confident that He is listening. I have to be willing to close my eyes to chaos, and look through eyes of faith to find peace and solace.

As the loved ones of service members we are still called to serve God. Questioning Him during deployments is a very human thing to do. It does not make us more distant from God, but allows God to draw us closer—just as He did with Job. ✪

God is with me when my husband is away, and with my husband when I am far from him.

SCRIPTURES

Deuteronomy 6:5-7
Love the Lord your God with all your heart and with all your soul and with all your strength. These commandments that I give you today are to be upon your hearts. Impress them on your children. Talk about them when you sit at home and when you walk along the road, when you lie down and when you get up.

Psalm 34:8
Taste and see that the Lord is good; blessed is the man who takes refuge in him.

Psalm 46:10
Be still, and know that I am God; I will be exalted among the nations, I will be exalted in the earth.

Proverbs 3:5-6
Trust in the Lord with all your heart and lean not on your own understanding; in all your ways acknowledge him, and he will make your paths straight.

Lamentations 3:21-23
Yet this I call to mind and therefore I have hope: Because of the Lord's great love we are not consumed, for his compassions never fail. They are new every morning; great is your faithfulness.

Romans 12:15
Rejoice with those who rejoice; mourn with those who mourn.

Galatians 6:9
Let us not become weary in doing good, for at the proper time we will reap a harvest if we do not give up.

Philippians 4:8
Finally, brothers, whatever is true, whatever is noble, whatever is right, whatever is pure, whatever is lovely, whatever is admirable—if anything is excellent or praiseworthy—think about such things.

Colossians 3:12
Therefore, as God's chosen people, holy and dearly loved, clothe yourselves with compassion, kindness, humility, gentleness and patience.

A LITTLE HELP FROM MY FRIENDS (AND FAMILY)

Taking Care of Myself

What are some practical ways you take care of yourself while your husband is gone?

Joanna: I spend some extra money on childcare! Yes, it's nice to save the deployment money, but the reason they pay it to you is because you need it. I had a college student come to my house twice a week for three to four hours so that I could have a break from the kids, take care of appointments for myself, send packages at the post office, or get a massage. My PWOC sisters were my resource people, especially the others who, like me, homeschooled. We had the flexibility to help each other out in a pinch—like when we suddenly made trips to the emergency room. We really took care of each other and supported each other through the difficult times.

Kim: I really enjoy the evenings, relaxing and maybe even pulling out a quick craft or something fun to do just for me. Sometimes I treat myself to take-out food or a special dinner and a movie. It is nice to treat yourself in small ways. I also work hard to find someone I trust to watch the children. It's important to get a breather every once in awhile. I've made a point of going out with my girlfriends—to dinner, a movie, shopping, or just playing games. And there are times when I've put all the kids to bed and had a babysitter come over for a short time just to get out by myself. ✪

Who Needs Help? Me?

God tells us to bear one another's burdens. But one of the challenges is to learn to accept help when we need it, or when someone loves us enough to offer. What is your experience?

Joanna: I've learned you're not supposed to be superwoman. You don't need to feel like you have to take care of everything and handle everyone's problems yourself. This is especially important if you are in some sort of leadership role in the unit. Delegate. Let people help you. Serve others and let them serve you. As military wives, we often feel like we have something to prove, to let people know "we can handle it" and we don't need others' help. This is so unbiblical, not to mention unhealthy. Make sure you have friends or family you can vent to—other than your husband. (Be sure not to bash on him!) Have people who will pray with you and help keep you spiritually and physically accountable (like reminding you to go to bed at a decent time).

Kim: God is definitely teaching me that it's okay to ask for help. I don't like to bother people. I feel like I've chosen my life and I need to take care of all areas. But God is teaching me about the body of Christ—and how to not only serve but also to *be served*. The "being served" is much harder for me than the serving. I'm learning that God wants to use other people in my life, and I need to humble myself and be thankful for the blessing.

Meredith: If you give the impression you don't need anything, people will stop offering. But when people made vague offers ("Let me know if you need anything") I would gratefully answer with specific, practical things they could do. This resulted in my having a designated parking spot at my church right outside the door, which really helped me get five young children safely in and out of church. It made the whole day much more worshipful. Also, for the first four months of Sundays, when we were in town, our family had Sunday lunch in the home of a family from church. It was a blessing to be with another family, see a dad in action, have one less meal to prepare, and share lives together. My church was such a source of support for us. Additionally, they prayed for us and provided free childcare at the church one day a month. The children were cared for by volunteers who prepared games, snacks, and lunch. They loved my children and me. It was invaluable. When ladies from our unit starting asking questions, I was able to invite them to my church, and these church friends were very welcoming to them as well. ✪

I've learned you're not supposed to be superwoman.

Encouraging Others

What would you say to a wife who is feeling "put upon" or neglected or fearful? How might you articulate that military families are a team? How can you encourage her in her faith?

Joanna: I'd tell her I understand how she feels because it is hard. Acknowledge her very valid emotions. Hopefully that can open the door to encouraging her in the Lord. Then bring it around to happy memories and funny things, and get her laughing about something. Maybe even mention something you're both looking forward to in the coming weeks.

We have a great opportunity to be a witness to God's power as we live out our Christian life in front of others who are without faith in Christ. There is a hope we possess and a peace that can be ours which speaks more loudly than sharing the four spiritual laws with someone. Our positive attitude and thankfulness in spite of difficulties will make people wonder what's different about us. There's also much that God wants to work in us and teach us during this time, if we're open to what He is trying to do (refining us and making us more like Christ).

Kim: I would encourage any military wife to be in a community with other military spouses, if possible. Military families have a special bond of understanding. There aren't many women who can do—or are asked to do—the things we do. When you know other military wives, you know they've been in your shoes. They've walked up the same steep hills and are stronger for it just as you will be. I know when I go back home to visit while my husband is gone, everyone feels sorry for me. After a while of so many people feeling sorry for me, I start to feel sorry for myself. Then I snap to and realize there is nothing to be feeling sorry about! God is faithful. The same God who calls us, equips us. He never leaves us. This is the time to stand on God's truths and hold tightly to His awesome promises. ✪

What Are Parents to Do?

by MG and Mrs. Don Riley, Army, United States

Together we have experienced one fifteen-month deployment of our son, and are once again looking to God for His sovereign protection as Darren begins another deployment to a combat zone. Yes, the anxiety is there, the unknowns are great, and we can do nothing about his situation—at least by ourselves. But we can, and do, seek God's loving embrace of Darren and his unit, and pray unceasingly that God will grant them safety, good health, strength, courage, and success in their mission. He is truly in God's hands now.

There were so many uncertainties as he began his first deployment. We were unsure of the environment and the type of operations he would be involved in. Our minds were full of questions: *How would he do? Would he try to be a hero? Would he stay healthy? Would he have access to e-mail or a phone?* We had some of these questions answered when we went to Fort Drum to bid him farewell and to meet a few of his unit leaders, but anxiety remained.

The two of us had very different feelings. Don was confident in the Army and Darren's unit leaders, and, although concerned, he felt great pride in knowing his son was going to fight for his country. Roz was watching her child go off into hostile territory. *Who would protect him?* This child whom she had nurtured and protected, hugged when sad, encouraged to discover new activities and interests, watched with amazement as he enjoyed exploring new things. A different emotion swells and dwells in a mother's heart when it is her son who marches off to battle, than if it were her husband.

We did the only thing we could do—trust wholly in God. We daily claimed the promises of Psalm 91, which we have posted in two locations in our home. We drew comfort from the words of David:

He who dwells in the shelter of the Most High will rest in the shadow of the Almighty. I will say of the Lord, "He is my refuge and my fortress, my God in whom I trust."

Even though television reports, radio alerts, news articles, and telephone calls would often startle us, we faithfully trusted in our all-sufficient Lord Jesus. Because Darren was stationed at a small patrol base in the mountains, he could only call or e-mail us every few weeks. Not knowing what might happen, and not wanting to think about the worst, we looked to God for comfort. We clung to Him even more as we learned that Darren was ▶▶▶

leading nightly patrols and experiencing frequent contact with enemy forces.

Surely he will save you from the fowler's snare and from the deadly pestilence. He will cover you with his feathers, and under his wings you will find refuge; his faithfulness will be your shield and rampart.

When we received the very sad news that one of Darren's closest friends was killed, we were overcome more by compassion—rather than fear—for the new widow, and for Darren. Although we were thankful the call we received wasn't about Darren, we grieved. Don went to Dover Air Force Base for the repatriation of his remains, and we attended the memorial service, then the funeral at Arlington.

You will not fear the terror of night, nor the arrow that flies by day, nor the pestilence that stalks in the darkness, nor the plague that destroys at midday. A thousand may fall at your side, ten thousand at your right hand, but it will not come near you. You will only observe with your eyes and see the punishment of the wicked.

For Darren's mid-tour leave the only thing he wanted to do was join a summer retreat session at OCF's Spring Canyon Conference Center in Colorado. We were overjoyed to be able to bring the entire family. Although the time with Darren was short, and we knew the return to Afghanistan would be mentally tough for a period, we remained excited to hear of his work and his challenges. And we prayed, and prayed, and prayed.

If you make the Most High your dwelling—even the Lord who is my refuge—then no harm will befall you, no disaster will come near your tent. For he will command his angels concerning you to guard you in all your ways; they will lift you up in their hands, so that you will not strike your foot against a stone.

Darren returned, and was disappointed to find out his platoon had fought some significant battles during his absence; so that made the reunion with his men more difficult. But he was soon back in the rhythm of daily weapons and equipment checks, soldier care and training, and continual patrols. Only a few months later, however, we received a call from Darren— he was wounded during a firefight. Darren sounded weak but, by the grace of God, the wounds were not critical. We did not take the news easily—unsettled by a mixture of fear and great thankfulness. We only wanted to physically be there with Darren, to comfort him, protect him, and suffer with him. But we couldn't. We trusted in God, and three weeks later he returned to his platoon where he wanted to be.

For Christmas, Darren revealed his heart, and only asked us to send him used clothing that he could pass out to poor villagers. We energized a lot of help for this, and finally Darren had to ask that we stop—the response from family and friends was overwhelming.

Don did not miss a day praying on his knees, early each morning, claiming the precious words of Psalm 91. Nights, however, were sometimes tougher than the days. Roz would frequently wake up in the middle of the night, compelled by the Holy Spirit to pray. Also Darren would often find his only time to call us was late at night our time. We, of course, would wake up and gladly listen and talk, pray with him, say good-bye, and pray again. As time went on we had fewer restless nights and we learned to lay even more of our parents' burden at God's feet.

Darren's homecoming was filled with joy beyond description, a peace that passes understanding, and the pride that only a parent can feel. We were excited to see him, hug him, and hear of his experience—and how he, too, placed his faith in God. And it was only with a small twinge of disappointment, but also enormous satisfaction in the way we raised him, to hear him say he "wouldn't mind going back again." He did not feel himself a hero, but humbly took satisfaction in doing his duty and helping the people, whom he came to love.

"Because he loves me" says the Lord, "I will rescue him; I will protect him, for he acknowledges my name. He will call upon me, and I will answer him; I will be with him in trouble, I will deliver him and honor him. With long life I will satisfy him and show him my salvation." ✪

A different emotion swells and dwells in a mother's heart when it is her son who marches off to battle, than if it were her husband.

Chasing Drake
When Grandparents Become Parents Again
by LTC James Karr, retired Army, Kansas

Today my wife, Laurel, and I find ourselves in an entirely new role. We have gone from being grandparents to being temporary parents. Our two-year-old grandson Drake has come to live with us while both of his parents are deployed for fifteen months. Two of our three daughters married Army men. And our son and his wife are also in the Army. Combined, they have served—or are serving—seven tours overseas, with several more expected.

Our dramatic metamorphosis from grandparents to parents started during the week before Easter, when we had planned to visit our son, Sam, and his wife, Sara, at Fort Campbell, Kentucky, to help them close up their house, and transfer Drake to our care in our home. We drove there expecting that everything would be in order, but the Army had moved up their deployments by four days, compressing their lives into a mad rush to depart and deploy.

Sara deployed on Easter Sunday. Sam reported after midnight and went wheels up Monday afternoon. When Sara had to do her final muster to be bussed to the holding area awaiting upload, it was one of the most heart-wrenching scenes we have ever witnessed. We joined hands in prayer and asked God to protect Sara, to help her do her duty well, and to bring her safely home again to her family. She tearfully gave Drake a series of tender kisses, then handed him over to Laurel, and kissed her husband good-bye. It really tore at my heartstrings to witness the separation of a wife and mom from her husband and only child. Yes, she knew what she was getting into when she raised her right hand in oath, but to see the reality of it was really tough. The tearful good-bye scene was repeated later that night as Sam departed.

The next few days were a blur. But somehow we arrived safely home with Drake. As we set up his crib in our home, we felt an overwhelming responsibility for his well-being. It is like being his parents, only different—he is our son and daughter-in-law's little boy, and we are his guardian protectors.

Drake has his moments when he asks for his mom and dad, but he doesn't dwell there. I think because we had him here for two months while Sam and Sara were on maneuvers it relieves some of the separation anxiety.

One of the most special times with Drake is at night when we say prayers with him for mommy and daddy—that God would keep them safe, and reunite all of us as a family again. Sam and Sara left us photo albums that we go through frequently. They also prepared video recordings of themselves reading Drake's favorite bedtime stories—a great way for him to stay connected to his mom and dad. After his bath each night, he bounces into bed with one last burst of energy before he begins to fade. He talks to mommy and daddy on TV, and then after the last story, when his dad tells him he loves him, Drake simply lays his head down and drifts off to sleep. His grandmother and I say one last prayer for him, and bless him good night.

While it is a sacrifice for us to change our lives to accommodate Drake, we do it gladly out of love for our children and for the Lord. It is important to be able to help keep the family together for support during these stressful times—especially when they are in combat or when their units cut communication to the outside because of casualties. These are the times when we gather as a family for prayer and sustainment, both for those at home and those abroad. The stress is palpable, but there is also a calm reassurance that God is in control.

We draw strength from Jeremiah 29:11: "'For I know the plans I have for you,' declares the Lord, 'Plans to prosper you and not to harm you, plans to give you hope and a future.'" God knows the future, and His plans for us are good and full of hope. This does not mean that we will be spared pain or hardship, but God will see us through to a glorious conclusion.

God bless all those in uniform serving overseas in harm's way—and their families serving at home. ▶▶▶

It really tore at my heartstrings to witness the separation of a wife and mom from her husband and only child.

These are things we found helpful for
Sam and Sara's deployment...

- Make sure wills are in place and updated.
- Make sure SGLI insurance is maxed up and
  beneficiaries are properly designated.
- Make sure all life insurance policies have been
  beneficiary reviewed.
- Make sure specific and general powers of attorney
  are prepared and executed.
- Make sure all medical records are ready for the
  child's guardians.
- Make sure DEERS and Tricare are notified and
  ready to accept the child at the new location.
- Make sure parents have left financial instructions
  and other important documents.
- Make sure POCs for Red Cross and units are
  known—with contact numbers.

In addition to clothes and favorite toys, be sure to
prepare and leave:
- Photo albums with lots of pictures of mom, dad,
  and child
- Recordings of the parents reading favorite bedtime
  stories

—Jim and Laurel ✪

Refreshment in the Rockies

by Colette Pappal, Army wife, Kansas

It is amazing that God gives you exactly what you need when you need it. My story begins with my move to Fort Leavenworth, Kansas, where we were assigned a home next to a Christian family. Little did I know that God already had His plan in motion. We had our household goods delivered to our new home, made some new friends, and started some roots again—as military families do.

My neighbor Amy asked my husband and me to be a part of a neighborhood Bible study. I was hesitant at first, but because we were such good friends, I said yes. But this invitation made me uneasy. I had never been to a Bible study, and didn't own a Bible. So, to say yes to a Bible study was a huge step for me. I had never talked to my husband or children about Christianity before. It had been over ten years since I had gone to church—and we had never gone as a family.

We studied a wonderful book called *Love and Respect* and it truly opened my eyes to the Christian life. During this Bible study, I got my first taste of prayer and fellowship. But before we could finish the study, my husband had to leave for his second year-long deployment. My Bible study facilitator suggested that I go to Spring Canyon for Heroes on the Home Front week. This was a week in the mountains of Colorado just for deployed spouses ▶▶▶

and their families. It sounded really wonderful. A few weeks later, I was offered a spot. I had no idea how dramatically Spring Canyon would change my life forever.

About one month after my husband's deployment we left for Spring Canyon. I had two girls: an eight-year-old and a seventeen-month-old. This seemed like a huge undertaking, for me to drive all the way to Colorado with two little children in the car. But I knew I needed to go.

After driving for twelve hours we finally made it to the entrance of Spring Canyon. At the entrance there is a large sign made out of wood that you drive under. At this exact moment my husband called to see if we were there yet. It was perfect timing. I almost started to cry. After we stopped at the office and checked in, it was a short drive through the woods and around the lake to our lodge. The scenery was amazing. The staff met us and helped unpack our things.

At thirty-four-years old I accepted Jesus as my Lord and Savior and finally felt at peace with myself—and with this deployment.

We were so pampered this week. I didn't have to cook or clean. My children were taken care of. It was a nice break from being a single parent during the deployment. I finally had time to focus on me. There were three other families staying in our lodge also. In total there were fourteen other families there. We all had our husbands deployed at this time. Everyone there made me feel so loved and accepted. I had never been in a group of Christian women before. It was amazing. There was so much encouragement and support. There was something different about them, and I wanted it too.

The first thing that had impacted me was the prayer. I had never been exposed to this kind of prayer in my life. I never had a personal relationship through prayer and I felt this personal relationship start to grow. The second thing that changed my spirit was the praise and worship music that we sang all week. It deeply touched me. Many of the songs that I heard at Spring Canyon have a special place in my heart. I shed many tears that week during prayer, many for my deployed husband and many for my new-found love of Jesus. I knew something was changing inside of me. The seed of faith was planted.

I truly had problems letting go and trusting what God had in His plans for me. I always thought I could do everything my way. I was wrong. I turned to God and I started to let Him direct my life. I accepted that I was "called" to be an Army wife and that this deployment was already in God's plan for my life. I now was relying on Jesus to get me through instead of doing it on my own.

The opportunity to go to Spring Canyon was the greatest blessing in my life. At thirty-four-years old I accepted Jesus as my Lord and Savior and finally felt at peace with myself—and with this deployment. After returning home from Spring Canyon, I started my new Christian life. I began going to the on-post chapel every Sunday and took a Christianity 101 class which answered many questions that I still had. My new sister-in-Christ, Michelle, supported me in prayer and helped me pick out my first Bible. I also joined Protestant Women of the Chapel (PWOC) and grew as a Christian through fellowship and Bible studies. I was baptized with four PWOC sisters by my side.

I know with my strong foundation that started at Spring Canyon, I now have a Protector who will see me through. It is amazing to me that this wonderful faith journey all started with a simple invitation to a Bible study and to Spring Canyon. ✪

Just Ask

by Becky Bolduc, Marine wife, Virginia

"Mom, the phone is ringing," my son yelled.

"I got it, buddy," I answered, "Hello."

"Hi, Becky, this is Joanne. I just wanted to call and tell you none of our guys were involved in the helicopter crash that is all over the news." We spoke for a few minutes about minor things, but I didn't pay attention to any of it, responding on instinct.

We said goodbye, I shut the door, and started sobbing. I was scared— more scared than I had ever been in my life. I had told everyone I could handle deployment. This was not our first separation; my husband had gone away frequently throughout his career, but he was never anywhere that required an "all clear" call before. What a wimp I was, one phone call and I was on the verge of hysterics.

I called my mother as soon as I could breathe and told her what had happened.

"Do you have church tonight?" she asked.

"Yeah, but I may just skip it. Too many questions won't help."

"Go. You need to be there."

"I really don't feel like it. I will be fine. It was just a shock, that's all." I was breathing again, but the fear was still wrapped firmly around my heart.

"Go. That's what the church family is for, helping you get through tough times."

"Okay, I'll go. I'll talk to you later. I love you—and thanks for listening."

"I love you, too. You can get through this. Just ask for some support." I realized she was right.

I was asked about Jeff as soon as I stepped in the church building. They all love him, too, and wanted to be reassured of his safety.

"What's wrong?" Bill asked.

"I just got word that the crash on the news was with one of the birds Jeff's unit supports. But none of the guys in our unit were hurt or even involved." I tried to be strong, but my throat closed up and my eyes filled with tears.

"Makes it real, huh?"

A weak "yep" was all I could manage. Then, "I don't even know why this has shaken me. Jeff is fine and I am a mess."

"Can I pray with you? Or *for* you?" Bill offered.

"Please, I don't even have the words right now," I said, gratefully accepting his offer, and thanking God for putting him in my family's life.

We sat down and prayed for the men and women overseas and particularly for Jeff and his unit. I felt a peace wash over me and I clung to it.

After dinner and service some of the ladies who are amazing prayer warriors cornered me. "What happened? You have been quiet all night, and you're trying to sneak out without us noticing." Lois knew me well.

"I got a rough call earlier saying that Jeff was not involved in the helicopter crash on today's news. It just hit me where Jeff is." I broke down again, overwhelmed by the powerful emotions.

"Let's go pray."

"Bill and I prayed for Jeff and his unit—as well as everyone else overseas. I'll be fine."

"Okay, let's go pray for you and the kiddos, and those of us left here waiting for them to come home," Sue, the pastor's wife, said pulling me into a room and shutting the door. Her prayers and reassurance were a blessing.

On the way out, Lois leaned over and repeated what she had been telling me for a while, "You've given it to God. Don't take it back!"

That evening, as I read my Bible, I was reminded of how the peace of God trumps all the anxiety that the world may offer. "Do not be anxious about anything, but in everything, by prayer and petition, with thanksgiving, present your requests to God. And the peace of God, which transcends all understanding, will guard your hearts and your minds in Christ Jesus" (Philippians 4:6-7). And I thanked God for brothers and sisters willing to pray with me—or *for* me—if I'll just ask. ✪

I was reminded of how the peace of God trumps all the anxiety that the world may offer.

The Blessings of Deployment

by Holly Hacker, Navy wife, Nebraska

Recently, at a women's retreat, the speaker encouraged us to jot down a list of hard times in our lives. The deployment my husband had just completed quickly went down on my list. Next, the speaker asked us to list what God brought out of that trial. What a great exercise that was! It can be so easy to focus on the negatives of deployment, complaining about its difficulties and challenges. Yet this simple exercise helped shift my thinking and helped me focus on a few of the many blessings God has given us *because of deployments*. There were the obvious blessings of unique ministry opportunities during the course of our deployment, but as I pondered the deployment as a whole I realized I had been blessed in many other areas as well.

The first blessing that came to mind was an experience that gave me a deeper understanding of God's goodness. It is so easy to equate God's goodness with the good things He's doing in our lives, rather than because His character *is* good. During my husband's first month at sea, our squadron had a fatal mishap. Shortly after that tragedy, God challenged my heart…had Tommy been one of the two pilots killed, could I truly stand and say, "God is good"? And rather painfully the blessings began.

Could I truly stand and say, "God is good" if Tommy had been one of the two pilots killed?

God refined my heart as a mother during Tommy's absence. He used this time "in the fire" to peel away layers of selfishness in me. As I yielded to His work, my relationship with our children grew even deeper. As homeschoolers, we spent all day, most every day, together during those long months. Rather than "driving me crazy" (although there were days I was certain I was headed there!), God redeemed that time and used it to knit our hearts together in a way that wouldn't have been possible otherwise. With Daddy away, we embarked on a 2000-mile road trip to see my parents and my in-laws. I can tell you there's nothing like ten hours in a minivan together to grow you close. These are blessings that will last a lifetime.

During the deployment I saw with new eyes just how much the body of Christ is needed. God humbled me as I had to ask others for help in various situations—something that had always been hard for me to do. Psalm 68:6 became a new reality to me: "God sets the lonely in families...." There were numerous times when loneliness crept in, particularly during holidays and on birthdays. When our family member was absent, God provided family in Christ to celebrate those special times with. These blessings carried me through the long journey of deployment.

A wonderfully unexpected deployment blessing I noted has been the relationship I enjoy with my in-laws. When Tommy was away, it forced me to develop my own relationship with his parents. They have supported me in his absence as much as my own parents. I've enjoyed numerous visits with them when he's been away and have learned things about them that not even their own son knew. My relationship with them is a blessing I'll always treasure.

The deployments have blessed my marriage. They force me to rely on the Lord for creative ways to support and encourage Tommy when he's away. Being a help-meet to your husband when he's halfway around the world definitely requires some inspiration from the Lord. Deployments also give me an opportunity to reflect on what a wonderful husband I have. During non-deployed times it's easy to get distracted by the busyness of everyday life and start taking one another for granted. With deployments, suddenly all of those things that used to annoy me seem so insignificant. This is a blessing I want to remember in the weeks and months ahead as life returns to "normal."

Each deployment is different and carries unique blessings just for you, blessings that can only come as a result of this deployment. I pray that you will be encouraged as you face your own separations from your spouse. ▶▶▶

Practical ways to support a family during deployment:

- Offer to mow their yard or wash their car—or even better, just show up on their doorstep one day and get to work.
- Invite them to join you on your family vacation.
- Take them a meal.
- Make a few "emergency casseroles" for their freezer or anonymously send them a gift card to a restaurant.
- Call them in the evening or on a weekend just to chat.
- Invite them to sit by you in chapel or at church.
- Offer to babysit.
- Ask on a regular basis, "Is anything broken in the house that we can fix for you?"
- Have them over for dinner on the weekend.
- Send a note of encouragement, letting them know how much you appreciate their spouse's service to our country.
- Pray for them—often. ✪

I Am Not Alone

by Wanda Marrero, Navy wife, California

Not long after moving to San Diego, my husband's ship left for six months plus. It was 0400 and my two children and I were in the shipyard saying goodbye to daddy. This was to be our first time apart for this long. My kids were too young to understand why mommy kept kissing daddy and could comprehend even less that daddy was going to be away for a long time. My three-year-old daughter kept asking, "Mommy, aren't we going home now?" I dreaded the idea of being apart and I did all I could to prolong our last few moments together. Finally, the moment had arrived and it was time for us to watch daddy walk up the brow of the ship. We stayed on the pier and watched the whole display of tugboats take his ship out of the bay and into the Pacific Ocean. No longer able to see the proud sailors standing on deck at attention, my nineteen-month-old son tugged on my shirt and said, "Daddy gone. I hungry. Go home."

Once home, we went about our business as usual. The kids went to preschool, and I went to work. That evening I prepared dinner, we played a few games, read a few stories, and I put the kids to sleep. Then in the quiet of our home it all hit me: *It's all up to me and I am all alone.* Even though my husband had gone through great lengths to make sure all would go smoothly during his absence, and all of our paperwork was in order, I became overwhelmed with fear of a different kind. Despite all of the reassurances at the pier that all will be okay, I suddenly realized the overwhelming responsibility I bore of protecting my children. Alone on my bed, the darkness and silence became the backdrop of loud clattering voices telling me how unsafe I was. *How can I protect my children if someone breaks into my home? How can I protect my children if there is an earthquake and the house collapses? What would happen if I died from a heart attack while I slept?* Satan was having a field day throwing all kinds of fearful scenarios my way.

Consumed with fear, I turned the light on and began to read my Bible. As part of my daily Bible reading, I make it a point to read through the Psalms and Proverbs every month. Each book contains such a rich diet of the nutrients I need for daily living that when I miss a serving my day seems incomplete. I read the chapter in Proverbs that corresponds with the day of the month. In Psalms I read five chapters every day to cover the 150 ▶▶▶

chapters it contains. I call it my one-a-day and my five-a-day.

While I read the first five chapters in Psalms my comfort was right around the corner waiting for me in Psalm 4:8. "I will lie down and sleep in peace, for you alone, O Lord, make me dwell in safety." Aaaahh, what peace I felt. That's right! The very God who protects our family when my husband is here will also protect us when he is not here. Just because my husband's body is stronger than mine, that does not mean that we are less safe when he is not around. My Lord is my strength! He is the hawk that watches over us and protects us from all evil. With Him at the helm I can lie down in security.

Twenty plus years of service later, and countless deployments under my belt, this Psalm is still my rock-a-bye song at bedtime. I am never alone, I am safe, and I am under His protection. As a seasoned veteran of deployments and separations, I have found myself sharing this verse with countless young wives through the years. Most precious to me was the day when I shared it with my daughter. She is now an adult woman and has a family of her own. Married to a Marine, it was not long till she discovered the reassuring power of Psalm 4:8 in her life. It's easy to think you are safe when you are in the arms of your husband. The reality is that your ultimate safety comes when you are cradled in the arms of the Lord. Next time you go to sleep, don't forget to give God a goodnight kiss and make yourself cozy on His lap. Sleep in the comfort of knowing that you are not alone. ✪

Consumed with fear, I turned the light on and began to read my Bible.

A Balancing Act

by Theresa Knapp, Marine wife, Colorado

Up until the time my husband deployed to go to war we had still maintained a hope that conflict could be avoided. But it couldn't. *What would be the consequences of this war?* That was on the mind of every spouse whose loved one would be heading into Iraq. Sure, I have endured deployments before, but not like this one. There was so much uncertainty—and the enemy was unconventional to say the least.

Prior to deployment there were many tearful nights and days thinking about our future. Once my husband left, I handed the situation completely over to God. He had always led and sustained me through all of my life—and this would be no exception.

I was the new key volunteer advisor for my husband's battalion, accountable for over seven-hundred spouses experiencing deployment. Managing the phone calls, the e-mails generated by our large core of volunteers, casualty notifications, and other tasks, was like a full time job. It kept me almost too busy to worry.

One day our daughter said to a family member, "Mom is always on the phone or on the computer." It caught me off guard—I had no idea that I had been neglecting our two children to this degree. So right then, I decided I would screen phone calls. If they could wait till morning, I would deal with them then. Also, all my computer work would be done while the children were at school or after they went to bed. I realized it was important for me to set a good example of coping, for I believed my children would pick up their emotional cues from me. When days were overwhelming and out of control, my motto was, "We will just do the very best we can." But most days we managed just fine, for our trust was in the Lord.

"I can do everything through him who gives me strength" became my well-oiled Bible verse (Philippians 4:13). My prayer life also improved as I prayed for my husband's safety, protection, health, and spiritual well being—and for all of our service men and women, and their families. I felt that I was contributing somehow through the power of prayer.

Perhaps the most difficult times I encountered were when our battalion suffered casualties. My heart ached for those families who had experienced the greatest sacrifice—the loss of a loved one. It was during those memorial ▶▶▶

services that I sensed a sacredness in how we in the military honor our dead.

What kept me going through this deployment were e-mails from Iraq, prayer, my family and friends who loved me through it all, and my very supportive church community. Actually, the most beneficial aspect was being able to assist other spouses who were also separated from their loved ones. God proved that He was there for us—no matter what happened. ✪

"I can do everything through him who gives me strength" became my well-oiled Bible verse (Philippians 4:13).

A Routine Day

by Beatrice Fishback, retired Army wife, United Kingdom

Jamie, a young wife and mother, stood quietly in the corner of the room where we would soon be meeting for our couple's Bible study. This evening, however, she attended alone. Not because of some disagreement with her husband, Josh. As a matter of fact I had recently seen them at the local BX, their hands interlocked like two high-school sweethearts. Jamie is alone—and will be for months to come—because Josh is now deployed. She is not unlike many other young adults in this community of U.S. military families here in Europe.

Fortunately, Jamie understands the importance of being a part of various programs where she gets emotional and spiritual support. She makes an effort to get involved with chapel, Bible studies, and reaching out to others, so that she doesn't focus on her loneliness—a loneliness that becomes more evident each time we meet. But Jamie not only has to cope with her feelings of isolation, she also bears the daily responsibility of caring for their young sons. Although Jamie is straining under the stress of being by herself, she carries a brave face and optimistic attitude.

Jamie and the many other American wives and mothers living in Europe, whose husbands are on active duty, deal with immense challenges—the most difficult being that they are thousands of miles from parents and extended family. Many live in cultures that are vastly different from the Wal-Mart or McDonald's familiarity we take for granted in the United States. Some are living on military installations; but many, if not most, live in a local foreign culture. These families are learning to speak another language and must learn how to read road signs while driving around unfamiliar territory. They are learning to cope with handling different currency and buying products carrying unfamiliar labels. The difference between their familiar life in America and where they now live sometimes appears subtle but can create major frustrations.

If you could take a slice of Jamie's day it would consist of routine moments filled with children's activities, running to and from school, dashing to the commissary, shopping, and other events demanding her attention. It's the part of the day *not* like the typical mother that sets Jamie and these ▶▶▶

other mothers apart. These young women eagerly await phone calls from their loved ones; many may not even know which country their active-duty spouses are calling from. The phone call may be the only contact they will have for days or weeks. Even today's instantaneous electronic connections can never replace the warmth of holding their spouse's hand.

Perhaps the hardest part of the day for military spouses—whether they are married to active duty members, National Guard, or Reservists—comes in the evening, when the children are asleep, neighbors are tucked into their own homes, and loneliness creeps in like a dark shadow. What they dread most is being alone with their thoughts. How could they not think of their loved one? Every evening, news stations march war headlines across the screen with blaring clarity. They worry about the world situation and how it impacts their family. Emotions and loneliness are their reality. Tomorrow will come, and along with it, another "routine day" of military life.

It is the American military family that is the strength of our nation.

Photo Courtesy of U.S. Navy // by Mass Communication Specialist 1st Class Leah Stiles/Released

It is the day-to-day, individual responsibilities which need to be taken into account—the maintenance and upkeep of homes, cars, lawn mowers, computers, and even vacuum cleaners. Duties normally shared at home now become the sole responsibility of one member of the family. There is a saying which goes, "Everything breaks, everything leaks, everything quits working when a spouse is deployed." Meanwhile the deployed member faces loneliness, deadly danger inherent in war, and feelings of anxiety about a spouse and a family left to fend for themselves.

Yet I have seen how these young families are coping and I am prouder to be an American today than I have ever been before. America's service men and women are among the best in the world, not only because of the quality of training they receive, but because they are sincere in their conviction of duty. Even more importantly—it is the American military family that is the strength of our nation. Without young women like Jamie and others, who are willing to wait for their husbands to come home, willing to "keep the home fires burning," our military would only be a skeleton—bones with no muscle to keep it moving.

We as Americans can and should be proud of our young military families. After all, they are living in other countries, giving up precious years and memories together as families—and some are laying down their lives. All of this in order for us to have the freedom to meet in our homes for Bible studies like the one Jamie attends. They sacrifice this, and more, so that we can experience freedom in the United States of America! ✪

How Deployment Worked for Me

by Sally Reinhard, Army wife, Colorado

This was our first deployment, and I was the brigade commander's wife. My husband had been TDY a lot, but this was our first long deployment—and both of our sons were teenagers. I knew I would need re-enforcements. We purposely sought out an OCF Bible study to be involved in, and these brothers and sisters were lifesavers as they prayed for us and really loved and encouraged us.

A friend from PWOC, whose husband was also deploying, suggested we start a support/prayer group for spouses of deployed soldiers. We met every other week during the lunch hour and just shared what was going on in our lives. This was where everyone felt safe to verbalize feelings and fears like, *What will I do if my husband is killed?* It's a perfectly normal question to consider during deployment, but something we all felt bad about admitting.

One lady in our group especially blessed me. She was a believer, this was her fifth deployment, and she had two teenagers. Her experience was invaluable, and her commitment to caring for soldiers' families unsurpassed.

My husband's unit is a bomb squad. In Iraq they did counter-IED (improvised explosive devices) work responding to calls to render IEDs safe and to investigate blasts. We are not a big group, with soldiers on different deployment schedules to different locations. All of them are well trained, but still the idea of this being their daily mission was not comforting. God knew my heart, and about a month before my husband left, He gave me this Scripture in my quiet time: "'Am I only a God nearby,' declares the Lord, 'and not a God far away? Can anyone hide in secret places so that I cannot see Him?...Do I not fill heaven and earth?' declares the Lord." (Jeremiah 23:23-24). I knew I could trust my husband to the God who sees everything. He is sovereign over Iraq, too. The irony of our soldiers going to Iraq, and Jeremiah writing about Babylon, was not lost on me.

Our guys deployed mid-November and our unit's first difficulty came a few days before Thanksgiving. Two of the NCO wives took care of the family in need beautifully. We all breathed a sigh of relief and thought *we can do this*. As time went on we all got into a routine and were managing.

As the deployment continued, I stayed involved with the other commanders' wives and attended all the ceremonies—and memorial services.

I lived on post and stayed involved with my neighbors; they were walking my path, and we understood each other's lives. God gave me lots of opportunities to encourage them—and they encouraged me. More importantly, I continued in Bible Study, PWOC, having my quiet time, and memorizing God's Word. At every ceremony I attended, when the national anthem was played, God reminded me to pray for the deployed soldiers, and for the wisdom of our leaders. For my husband, God gave me 1 Chronicles 12:32 to pray for him, that he would be like the men of Issachar, "who understood the times and knew what Israel should do."

Life was going along fairly well until the news leaked of a three-month extension. Unfortunately, it came as a surprise to everyone, including the commanders in theatre. I felt bad for my husband—and worse for me. By this time our older son, a senior in high school, was really wanting out from under my authority. I was blessed to have a godly friend who kept in close contact with me and encouraged me in the Lord daily. She committed to seeing me every quarter while Karl was deployed. This was of unbelievable encouragement to me—another adult to talk to, who knew my kids and who would speak the truth in love.

Mid-tour did come! Karl and I took four days and went to the mountains alone—which was a very good decision. He was exhausted, and it helped him to be away from the house, his headquarters, and the boys for a little while. It was harder to say good-bye this time because we knew this wasn't really mid-tour, and we wouldn't see him for many months.

But through it all, God made it very clear that He is in total control of every detail. There is no such thing as an accident, coincidence, or random event. God is control of our lives and our world. ✪

'Am I only a God nearby,' declares the Lord, 'and not a God far away?'

Photo Courtesy of U.S. Army // by Sgt. Nathan J. J. Hoskins, 1st ACB, 1st Cav. Div. Public Affairs

Chapter 5

SCRIPTURES

Psalm 37:4-5
Delight yourself in the Lord and he will give you the desires of your heart. Commit your way to the Lord; trust in him and he will do this.

Zephaniah 3:17
The Lord your God is with you, he is mighty to save. He will take great delight in you, he will quiet you with his love, he will rejoice over you with singing.

John 6:68
Simon Peter answered him, "Lord, to whom shall we go? You have the words of eternal life."

John 13:14
Now that I, your Lord and Teacher, have washed your feet, you also should wash one another's feet.

2 Corinthians 1:3-4
Praise be to the God and Father of our Lord Jesus Christ, the Father of compassion and the God of all comfort, who comforts us in all our troubles, so that we can comfort those in any trouble with the comfort we ourselves have received from God.

Galatians 6:10
Therefore, as we have opportunity, let us do good to all people, especially to those who belong to the family of believers.

Philippians 2:4
Each of you should look not only to your own interests, but also to the interests of others.

Hebrews 10:25
Let us not give up meeting together, as some are in the habit of doing, but let us encourage one another—and all the more as you see the Day approaching.

1 Peter 5:7
Cast all your anxiety on him because he cares for you.

HOME AGAIN!

Honey, I'm Home!

Any advice for reunions/re-entry?

Joanna: I felt like it was important for only our family to be there, so we didn't invite the parents or in-laws to the welcome home ceremony. It's hard enough to readjust to being a family again without having to share him with everyone. The kids especially needed that time with him. There is plenty of time to visit family during leave time after they get back.

Kim: This is the best part of the deployment. How many married couples can get butterflies, sweaty palms, and become all nervous again? Those are all the fun feelings you get to experience when going to the big Homecoming Day.

The flip side is when the honeymoon is over! It can be hard to go from being the decision maker, head finance person, disciplinarian, the one in charge, and then back to being the second in command. It is hard to fall back and let some of the responsibilities go. It is hard for me to hear, "No, I don't think we should do that," or "No, we really don't need to buy that." I sometimes felt like I had reverted to being a child. Yet it was nice to be free of some of the responsibilities, and I was happy to pass them off. I needed to remind myself that God calls me to submit.

It's a huge adjustment for those couples who have had a baby while they were separated. I had a friend who had their first baby while her husband was deployed, and he was coming home when the baby was already a few months old. She was into her routine. I tried to remind her gently that the baby was his, too. He might not know her exact way of doing things, but there is usually more than one way to get the job done. Be thankful for his care and teach him gently as you go along. Most of all, be an encourager in this new chapter of his life! ✪

Reflections: We Did It!

Looking back on deployments, what are some perspectives you can pass along?

Kim: My saying is that deployment is a time I try not only to survive but to thrive! I don't always measure up, but it's a great place to start—and it gets me through some of the tough times.

Joanna: In the end, I do feel like there were times when we were just "surviving" (and that's okay, too). Sometimes it's hard to deal with lots of little ones and maintain a focus on what God wants to do in this because you are just plain exhausted. But God understands that and works anyway, giving us a great testimony through certain trials. Sometimes it's just the "nuts and bolts" of living that get us up in the mornings.

Meredith: During our deployment, my husband was a company commander and I was the FRG (Family Readiness Group) leader. Although it was a lot of responsibility, it was really helpful for me because Matt and I had such a shared sense of calling. God had called us to this challenge and He would take care of our family. I felt strongly that I needed to care for the families in our unit and lead them through this gracefully. I really thought about what should be different in my life because of my faith. I realized that we were all hoping for the same things: that our soldier would come home safely and that we'd do a good job on the home front. But I knew, too, that I had a greater hope. Even if my husband didn't return, I had an unchanging hope, a certainty. God was in control. I did have to remind myself of this truth throughout, but it was a bedrock for me.

Matt and I both felt very strongly that this was the challenge to which God had called our family. Matt wanted to lead his men with wisdom and courage and integrity. I wanted to walk through the challenge of caring for our family and the families of our soldiers in such a way as to give an answer for the hope that I have in Jesus. We feel very thankful to have had this opportunity. Throughout the year, we saw God provide for us and for our children. We also feel very thankful that God used so many of our friends and family to lift us up and see us through. ✪

Drawn to God through Struggles

by Julie Self, former Army wife

A lot has changed since…that first time butterflies filled my stomach when Nathan Self invited me over to watch a movie at his house. As a naïve fifteen-year-old, I could not have imagined that our innocent puppy love would grow into a deep, abiding faith in each other, a commitment so strong that no amount of loneliness, war, or hurt could ever separate us. Fifteen years after that first date, I see that God has been the key to our life together.

Army marriages are not easy, and ours was no exception. We spent our first married year separated by schooling commitments. Once we were together, I still spent time alone, with his weeks in the field, early mornings and late nights, and three deployments. But despite our personal desire to spend more time together, we loved serving our country. We had fallen in love with the Army and with the American Soldier.

Just more than a month after 9/11, Nathan and I welcomed our first child, Caleb, into the world. I fell in love again with Nathan—this time as my son's father, not just as my husband. I'll never forget seeing Nathan hold Caleb for the first time in the hospital rocking chair and feeling overwhelmed with gratitude.

Nathan deployed to war…two days after we quietly celebrated our first Christmas as parents. I had more worries and fears on this deployment than on the previous one…. It was war, and I had a baby to take care of. During ▶▶▶

Now I saw that God had given me an additional gift—a piece of Nathan to hold while he was away.

the many late-night hours of nursing a newborn, I prayed for Nathan's safety and well-being.... He and I had worried about bringing a child into such an uncertain world when Caleb was born, but now I saw that God had given me an additional gift—a piece of Nathan to hold while he was away. And I learned to hold on to God more and more.

I discovered during our time apart that when I had been fortunate enough to have Nathan with me every day, it was easy to take his presence for granted. I hadn't told him the things I most deeply needed or wanted to tell him. But when Nathan was overseas, we communicated through e-mail, letters, and occasional phone calls, and there was no holding back. We were clear and up-front about our fears in life and our feelings for each other. During those times, I found the same to be true with my relationship with God. I relied on Him in all my fears, doubts, loneliness—everything. And every time the Lord brought Nathan home to me, I wanted to continue that feeling of "no holding back," that wonderful, vulnerable dependence we had developed when we were apart.

But the aftermath of war brought challenging and difficult times at home. After Nathan came home for good, he started to really experience the emotional effects of having been in war—something that neither of us saw coming. He never talked with me about his deployed experiences. He withdrew from me and, somehow, from himself. It was heartbreaking. Nathan had always been so strong. To see him at a breaking point—to see anyone I loved in pain—was not easy. Where was the Nathan I had married? I wanted the problems to disappear and be fixed right away. I wanted to fix them myself. But I couldn't.

At times, we were desperate. But in our desperation, we sought the Lord—and He was there. We got on our knees at night and simply laid ourselves and our feelings before God. We asked for His help. We looked for answers in the Bible. We also journaled to each other regularly and worked through our feelings that way. We were vulnerable, and we communicated our hurts and frustrations. We learned to forgive both ourselves and each other. By God's grace and mercy, we were able to heal.

God never promised an easy life free from trials and tribulations. He did, however, say that He would never leave us or forsake us. It is during these difficult times that we can become the people God wants us to be. When faced with such challenging events in this life, we have a choice. We can become bitter, resentful, or angry and eventually give up or run away. Or we can choose to be obedient: to love unconditionally, to forgive, and to heal.

Much has changed for us. We are no longer in the Army, and war has altered us, as it has for so many others, in ways that cannot be ignored. At times, I didn't want to go through any of it. I didn't care whether God had a purpose in all of it; I said, "No, God, this is not what I asked for." There was a time when I rejected the changes, when I just wanted my old life back. But I've seen God bringing about even greater changes in me. I've reached a point where I see that it's possible to be joyful even in the midst of trials, in knowing that God is in control. I've reached a point where I love my soldier without qualification—regardless of his wounds, whether seen or unseen. And I love him, regardless of the ways he may have wounded me. I have felt the joy of knowing that even though circumstances change and people change, God stays the same.

Scripture says that "God causes everything to work together for the good of those who love God and are called according to His purpose for them" (Romans 8:28, NLT). Nathan and I look back now and see that during those dark days, we were being drawn to God. He truly did cause our struggles to work together for our good—for the good of our relationship with Him and for the good of our marriage.

God has since blessed us with two more beautiful children. Nathan and I are excited that we can one day share our story with them, in hope that they, too, will choose to follow Jesus even through struggles and pain, for He is the solution to our struggles and the ultimate Healer of our pain.

Nathan, I am blessed to be called your bride. I thank you for the love, devotion, strength, and tenderness you give to our family. I look forward to growing old with you. You still give me butterflies. ✪

Re-entry Reminders

by Ilene Stubbs, retired Army wife, Florida

- Normal has changed for everyone.

- Be patient—it takes time to get into a routine.

- Soldiers haven't been on a vacation.

- Expect your household to be different.

- Keep life as routine as possible.

- Take time to re-adjust to one another.

- Go slow.

- Communicate feelings.

- Anxiety is normal.

- Discuss frustrations.

- Accept that we are all different.

- Initial discomfort adjusting doesn't mean your spouse is unhappy with you or the family.

- Communicate ahead of your spouse's return about radical changes in your physical appearance (once a redhead now a blonde).

- Communicate about changes in discipline of children.

- Assume you've both been faithful to one another unless strong evidence indicates differently. Then seek wise counsel.

- Be open about changes that have occurred in your life—spiritually, emotionally, and physically.

- Avoid "who had it worse games."

- Remember intimacy and sex are not the same thing.

- Accommodate, accommodate, accommodate. Meet small requests—like eating favorite food three times a day.

- Listen, look, listen.

- Take it easy. Let things happen naturally.

- Old problems don't disappear.

- Take time to share expectations and concerns before your spouse returns home.

- Soldiers' sleeping patterns may vary.

- Spouses may need space—let them have as much time as needed.

- Realize you will never understand all your spouse has been through.

- Military spouses may have nightmares. Don't panic.

- If a soldier doesn't want to talk, don't push.

- Re-union is difficult! Stay calm and **don't give up!!**

"Finally, all of you, live in harmony with one another; be sympathetic, love as brothers, be compassionate and humble." —1 Peter 3:8 ✪

Realize you will never understand all your spouse has been through.

A Refuge

by Nashawn Turner, Marine wife, Virginia

It was 2:30 in the morning, a time when anyone would dread getting a call. This was not a call to say that a loved one has been badly hurt or that someone just passed away. No, this call was like none other. It was "The Call"—the unexpected call, the call of duty, **the call to war.** It was the call that no military wife is ever quite prepared for her husband to answer.

The feeling that came over me that night was not only a feeling of sadness, but also a wave of fear, uncertainty, and loneliness. At that very moment, it felt like the bottom dropped out of my life. My husband had just one hour to report for duty. The only thing we could do was to surrender the situation to the Lord and trust that all would be well. My husband and I embraced each other, verbalized our love for one another, and then prayed.

Emotionally, I was all over the map. But soon I was reminded of what Psalm 61 says about God being the ROCK that is higher than I, the refuge and strong tower. As I began to accept what was taking place in my life, "my call" as the spouse left behind became clearer. Just as my husband took an oath to support and defend our great country, I, too, pledged my allegiance to the covenant of our marriage and life as a military family—with all it entails. I had to step up to the plate by standing tall and strong in my call to support and encourage my husband, and to assure my children that everything was going to be all right. I had to let my husband know that we were going to be OK, and that I was anointed to fulfill this assignment with courage. Because of my faith in God, I knew that I could do all things through Christ who strengthens me (Philippians 4:13). Although I knew that it would be a tough road ahead, I was reminded of how the Bible declares that God's grace would prove to be sufficient for me during this time in my life and His strength would be made perfect in my weakness (2 Corinthians 12:9).

After my husband's departure, I felt alone and lost. Although I wanted to lock myself up in the room and just stay in the bed, I knew I had to push through everything I was feeling because of my children. They needed me more than ever.

As I began to place my hope and trust in the Lord, I began to experience God's blessed assurance that everything was going to be all right. Through prayer and reading the Word of God daily, I grew stronger in my faith and became more intimately acquainted with God in a way that I had never known Him before.

I began to journal my journey.

I began to journal my journey. I will never forget a powerful word God spoke to me as I cried out to Him in prayer. As I waited in silence before Him, I wrote down what He spoke to my spirit that day. "Make a commitment to meet with Me daily. It's not so much the outside pressures, but the pressures from within that are coming against you greatly. Surrender is the key. You can't control life, you can only manage it. However, managing it in peace comes from trusting and relying on Me. It comes from casting all of your cares on Me and letting Me care for them. Your peace is based on how much you will trust Me and look to Me alone. I know where you are and I know how to bring you to where you need to be. Let Me take you through the process. Good things are ahead and a better way of handling things is at hand. Don't allow yourself to become overwhelmed. Often take refuge in Me to find shelter from the storm. For I will prove how My grace is sufficient for you. It is all that you need and it is more than enough to cause you to triumph over anything."

My family, church family, and many friends also helped me through this process by praying for me. They blessed me with exactly what I needed—a hug, a shoulder to cry on, a gift card for a massage or meals so I didn't have to cook that day, or a baby sitter for my children so I could go see a movie and just laugh. They were wonderful! I really saw the love of Jesus in action.

I also came to realize that the love that my husband and I have for each other would see us through. We had to believe that our family would survive this—and not just survive—but thrive after all this was over.

While my husband was gone, we stayed in constant touch with one another via cards, letters, recorded messages, pictures, and little tokens ▶▶▶

that reminded us of our love. We were determined that in spite of his deployment, we would work hard at staying connected. There were times when I would miss his phone call and I would be so disappointed, and hoped he would call back again. He always left a message and I would play that message over and over again just to hear his voice.

Nothing could compare to the moment when I found out that Keith was coming home earlier than expected. I praised God for such good news! It was one of my greatest moments. The kids and I made a huge "Welcome Home" sign that we placed on the garage. The kids drew pictures of themselves with a personal message for daddy from each of them.

My husband and I discussed his homecoming and the fact that he really wanted to have just one night alone with me. So I made arrangements for the children to spend the night at a friend's house. I bought fresh, delicious, juicy fruit, created a wonderful fruit display on a beautiful crystal tray, and laid it on top of the bed. I had candles and flowers placed around the bedroom.

When I went to pick him up on the military base, I could not believe that this day had finally arrived. I was nervous and excited all at the same time. And when I saw him step off the bus, it felt like all my dreams had come true—he was finally HOME!!! It was a day and night we will never forget. When the children saw him the following day, they were surprised and overjoyed. They just cried and cried, which also made me cry with them. We were one big happy family again for the moment.

Following my husband's return home, it took him a while to get adjusted to being home again. He did not know quite where he fit in anymore. Though I was anxious for him to tell me what actually happened over there, he really did not have much to say. It seemed as if he wanted to leave it all over there and deal with just the here-and-now.

At first that bothered me, then I remembered from some of the re-entry briefing information I had read, that sometimes it could take a while for a spouse to open up. I had to learn to be patient with him and just let him share when he was ready. I also had to allow him to adjust to getting back into family life at his own pace instead of trying to push our everyday routine at him and expecting him to just jump in and take over.

Looking back on this deployment, I see how prayer and God's Word rescued my husband from danger—seen and unseen—and gave me a peace that surpassed all my understanding. I found out that trusting in God made all the difference when walking through such a hard trial, but I MADE IT! ✪

Strength and Tears

Anonymous

My wife and I recently attended my brother-in-law's welcome home celebration from his deployment. While we waited for the soldiers to arrive we listened to loud, patriotic tunes and watched giant slide presentations of these heroes in action. With the crowd whipped to a suitable froth, the troops marched into the gymnasium and after an amazingly short speech by the commanding general, they were released to their families. It was an incredible sight, and from the sheer volume an unknowing passerby outside the building might have thought March Madness was upon us.

Next to us in the stands sat a young woman whose husband had been killed in the war. She was there to support her friends, especially my brother-in-law and his wife. Their friendship had begun at an OCF Bible study during the officer basic course, and continued at their first duty station. Off to the side, her steady tears revealed the pain of watching others reunite while knowing she would have no earthly opportunity to do this herself.

Our military community is truly extraordinary. The spectrum of emotions that evening reminded me of that. Normal people asked to do extraordinary things: leave your family for a year, take care of small children and a home by yourself, go to a foreign land and knowingly drive on roads watched by snipers, and carry on in life without the one you love the most.

It is comforting to know that our friend in the stands that evening and her husband both know Jesus as their Savior, so their separation is only temporary. Please continue to pray for all of our service men and women and their families—especially those who have made the ultimate sacrifice. ✪

It was an incredible sight.

SCRIPTURES

Psalm 40:5
Many, O Lord my God, are the wonders you have done. The things you planned for us no one can recount to you; were I to speak and tell of them, they would be too many to declare.

Proverbs 5:18
May your fountain be blessed, and may you rejoice in the wife of your youth.

Proverbs 13:12
Hope deferred makes the heart sick, but a longing fulfilled is a tree of life.

Romans 15:32
. . . so that by God's will I may come to you with joy and together with you be refreshed.

Ephesians 3:20-22
Now to him who is able to do immeasurably more than all we ask or imagine, according to his power that is at work within us, to him be glory in the church and in Christ Jesus throughout all generations, for ever and ever! Amen.

Philemon 1:7
Your love has given me great joy and encouragement, because you, brother, have refreshed the hearts of the saints.

3 John 1:13-14
I have much to write you, but I do not want to do so with pen and ink. I hope to see you soon, and we will talk face to face.

Afterward

"God himself deeply loves soldiers. His own Son, in fact, was the ultimate Warrior—shedding his blood, absorbing the enemy's blows, laying down his life for his friends. No greater love. This same Jesus will be back one day astride a great warhorse, wearing a bloodstained robe, and carrying a sword.

A man today, like so many prominent men in the Bible, can be both a physical warrior and a spiritual warrior at the same time. The two are not exclusive. Neither compromises the other."

—Stu Weber

Walking in the Spirit

A Prayer for Military Wives

May Jehovah, the great God of love, joy, peace, patience, kindness, goodness, faithfulness, gentleness and self-control, bless you with His LOVE—and with each of these attributes that will strengthen you and touch the lives of everyone you meet.

JOY...when emails or phone calls are late in coming, and when birthdays or anniversaries are forgotten.

PEACE...in the midst of complaining children and crashing computers.

PATIENCE...when people let you down.

KINDNESS...when your husband gets promoted, but your friends do not.

GOODNESS...when the commander's spouse calls at the last minute for help with a unit event.

FAITHFULNESS...when you begin to doubt the strength God has given you to go on.

GENTLENESS...when the baby has been crying all night and needs your loving touch one more time.

SELF-CONTROL...when the kids are sick, dinner has burned, and you receive a call that your husband's deployment has been extended.

May you walk with the inner strength that comes from the LOVE of Christ Jesus.

—*Karen L. Martin*

This book was built on the foundation of its predecessor *Deployed Not Disconnected*, edited by Don and Karen Martin, which has been an inspiration to deployed service men and women for many years. OCF acknowledges the Martin's significant contribution to helping deployed families thrive.

Officers' Christian Fellowship (OCF) is a non-denominational Christian organization that ministers to the entire military society. OCF exists to glorify God by uniting Christian officers for biblical fellowship and outreach, equipping and encouraging them to minister effectively in the military society.

What we do:
- Assist Christians in the integration of their faith and witness into their professional military life.
- Assist chaplains in cultivating a healthy spiritual environment in the military through an active Christian presence and ministry.
- Provide local military fellowship through small-group Bible studies, a professional magazine, and two national conference centers for periodic enrichment and refreshment.
- Provide support to families through home fellowship groups, and to provide support to spouses and children when military members are deployed.
- Provide a network of military Christians at U.S. installations worldwide.
- Strengthen the spiritual dimension of professional military leadership.

Throughout this book, several authors have mentioned Spring Canyon and White Sulphur Springs. These are Christian camp and conference centers owned by Officers' Christian Fellowship (OCF). Spring Canyon is in the Rocky Mountains just west of Buena Vista, Colorado. White Sulphur Springs is in the Allegheny Mountains just outside Manns Choice, Pennsylvania. While the two locations offer very different settings, every event offered year-round is covered in prayer and designed to encourage and strengthen military families.

Explore www.ocfusa.org for more information on these conference centers, or any other aspect of Officers' Christian Fellowship and our ministry to the military society.

Spring Canyon

The *Thriving, Not Just Surviving* articles listed below have been adapted from articles previously printed in publications by Officers' Christian Fellowship—or other ministries—as indicated.

Chapter One

Daddy, I Don't Want You to Go — Cindy Wesley — COMMAND magazine

Begin with the End in Mind — Bobbie Simpson — OCF Family Outreach materials

Chapter Two

God's Plans Prevail — Christy Kaiser — COMMAND magazine
Also printed in *Finding Hope Beyond the Battle: A Bible for Military Families*. Used with permission from International Bible Society.

Double Duty for a Solo Spouse — Marshéle Carter Waddell — COMMAND magazine
Adapted from *Hope for the Home Front*
Used with permission from One Hope Ministry

Share My Calling — Anne Borcherding — COMMAND magazine

Chapter Three

Daddy's Letter to Son — LTC Frank Gray, USA — COMMAND magazine

The Sacrifice for Rebirth in Iraq — Capt Rob James, USMC — COMMAND magazine

I Have Met Some Great Heroes — CPT Kristine Varga, USA — COMMAND magazine

Ordinary People... — MAJ David Segulin, USA — CONNECTED newsletter

Shepherd of Warriors — CH(CPT) Don Williamson, USA — CONNECTED newsletter